Also by Michael Keene

BOOKS

Folklore and Legends of Rochester

Murder, Mayhem & Madness

Question of Sanity

Mad House

Abandoned

FILMS

The Murder of William Lyman

The Strange Disappearance of Captain William Morgan

In Search of White Crows

The Code of Handsome Lake

Visions

AUDIO BOOKS

Anthology

THE PSYCHIC HIGHWAY

How the Erie Canal Changed America

Michael T. Keene (signature)

Michael T. Keene

WM

Published by Willow Manor Publishing

Fredericksburg, V.A. 22406

www.willowmanorpublishing.com

Illustrations courtesy of Ad-Hoc Productions

Cover image Pittsford on the Erie Canal. 1837 by George Harvey

Courtesy of Fenimore Art Museum, Cooperstown, NY

First published 2016

Manufactured in the United States

LCCN 2016931223

Library of Congress Catalogue-in-Publication Data

Keene, Michael.

The Psychic Highway: How the Erie Canal Changed America

Michael Keene

p.cm.

Includes bibliographical references.

ISBN 978-1-939688-32-3

1.History—New York (state). 2. 19th Century—New York (state) 3. The Erie Canal.
4. The Underground Railroad. 5. Women's Rights—New York (state).

Anecdotes. I. Title

CONTENTS

October 27, 1825, the Seneca Chief approaches the stone aqueduct in Rochester:

"Who comes there?"

"Your brothers from the West, on the waters of the Great Lakes."

"By what means have they been diverted so far from their natural course?"

"Through the channel of the Erie Canal."

"By whose authority and by whom was a work of such magnitude accomplished?"

"By the authority and enterprise of the people of New York."

Foreward

Look up the Wikipedia article origin of *"The Empire State"* and you'll find a number of theories for the source of New York's official motto. In Michael Keene's latest book, *The Psychic Highway*, he does not weigh in on any particular explanation; he just gives us countless reasons for making the claim and in so doing, presents us with a unique insight into the origins and consequence of the Erie Canal.

Some of us might trace our ancestry back to the earliest days of New York. But the earliest of our line would be relative newcomers as Keene begins his story of the history of the Erie Canal that he purports to have begun during the great ice age, nearly two million years ago!

None of us are descended from that early life for good reason - there were only roots, trees, peat grasses and other plant forms, that appeared during this period. These natural growths would provide sustenance for the next round of 'New Yorkers'—the mastodons, mammoths, saber-toothed tigers and giant ground sloths that came to dominate what is now New York State.

After the prehistoric arrival of plants and beasts, Keene tells of the continent's first humans, the Clovis People, who made their appearance by trekking across the northwestern continental strait into North America from Central Europe. In subsequent millennia's the Clovis were replaced by the Lamokas, then the Hopewells, the Lenapes, and finally followed by the Iroquois.

During the age of discovery beginning during the 15th century, Keene then introduces us to the great explorers; Giovanni Verrazano who discovered New York Bay, Jacques Cartier, who approached northern New York from the territory he assigned the name Canada, and Henry Hudson, who traveled north up the river that would bear his name.

In the 18th and 19th centuries we learn of the visionaries such as the brilliant Robert Fulton inventor of the steam boat, the first to recommend the construction of a canal that would stretch from the Hudson River to Lake Erie, and the mercurial Jesse Hawley who while sitting in debtors prison conceived of how this canal could be built and offered in unbelievable detail, the plans for its reality.

Of this period Keene writes, *"This powerful waterway carried a flotilla of radicals, visionaries, social reformers, and prophets bent on the idea of creating a new society. It was as if a bolt of electricity struck Western New York lighting it up as fertile ground for ideas and lifestyles that had never been expressed or attempted before".*

"It delivered people to important places for important reasons, like Susan Cady Stanton and Lucretia Mott to Seneca Falls for history's first women's convention, to Rochester to meet and support abolitionists Frederick Douglass and Harriett Tubman, or to witness the Fox Sisters summon spirits and their eerie knockings. Or maybe people on the temperance bandwagon hurrying to the Burned Over District so Charles Finney could save their souls".

These were, indeed, people of great mental and spiritual acuity to conceive of such ideas and bringing them to fruition made possible with the Erie Canals final glorious completion. Where there is progress, there is change, economically and socially. Because of the Erie Canal, New York State didn't simply eke its way into historic transformation; it exploded into the 19th century in ways that galvanized all aspects of American life".

David C. Minor, Canal Society of New York

Part One

PRE-HISTORY

Chapter 1

Climate Change

Colossal, bigger-than-life creatures lived, multiplied and reigned over the places we now call home, in an environment that was far from ideal. They slept and wakened, foraged for food and nourishment, fought off greedy intruders, protected their young, and staked claim to their established territories until they perished naturally or were killed by their own—or by man.

Fierce saber-toothed tigers, huge giant ground sloths, towering mammoths, and mastodons lived throughout and populated New York State. They were, indeed, our original neighbors.

These giant mammals called *"megafauna"* (translated from "large animal") lived, adapted, and survived in the terrain formed by the Great Ice Age 1.8 million years ago and by subsequent "mini" ice ages. The last of these glacial periods occurred approximately 70,000 years ago.[1]

It's hard to imagine the size and strength of these prehistoric denizens. The popular animated *Ice Age* films give a lighthearted glimpse into their grueling existence and how they survived each day:

Sid (the sloth): Hey, what's your problem?

Manny (the mammoth): You are my problem.

Sid: Well, I think you're stressed, and that's why you eat so much. I mean, it's hard to get fat on a vegan diet.

Manny: I'm not fat. It's all this fur. It makes me look... poofy.

Sid: Fine. You have fat hair. But when you're ready to talk, I'm here. You know? This whole ice age thing is getting old. You know what I could go for? A global warming.

Meet the Neighbors

Saber-toothed tigers ate meat and dined on species of prehistoric horses and bovine populations, or cow-like animals. Along with the woolly mammoth, the saber-toothed tiger was the most famous megafauna mammal of the Pleistocene epoch.

This beast, Smilodon fatalis, descended from the prehistoric cat, not the tiger. It gained a ferocious reputation from its high-mounted, curving canines. In the largest of the species, canines could measure an imposing 12 inches. These grizzly weapons, however, were brittle and easily chipped, broken, or even demolished in close combat. The teeth never grew back. Smilodon also possessed weaker jaws than other cat species of equal size and weight. Because of these factors, it honed a specific major hunting technique, remaining in the lower branches of trees and pouncing on prey, while sinking the saber teeth into the animal's neck leading it to bleed to death.[2]

The giant ground sloth (*Megalonyx jeffersonii*) failed to gain a title until Thomas Jefferson named it in 1797 after examining bones found in a West Virginia cave. Megalonyx means "giant claw". This species inhabited an enormous area ranging from the West coast, as far north as Alaska, and through most states east of the Rocky Mountains. The sloth's diet consisted mainly of insects and plant roots. The front legs of this bulky, furry, 8 to 10-foot-long creature grew longer and more muscular than its rear limbs. Its huge front claws adapted to grab large clumps of vegetation. The sloth maintained the ability to rise up in a semi-erect position to feed on tree leaves, using its massive front claws to strip branches clean, despite weighing as much as 800 pounds.

Mastodons were the prototype for the elephant, as we know it, today. The American mastodon (*M. americanum*) traveled more than any of its species, particularly in North America and along the east coast into New England with higher concentrations in what would become the Mid-Atlantic States.

These social behemoths lived in mixed herds or groups of adult females and their young. As males reached sexual maturity, they abandoned their herds

Climate Change

Many of the saber-toothed cats' food sources were large mammals such as elephants, rhinos, and other colossal herbivores of the era.

to either live alone or in male bonded groups. Mastodons survived on plants and grassy vegetation, browsing and grazing in their travels.

The Cohoes Mastodon

Evidence of the mastodon's existence in New York State brought attention to the city of Cohoes in 1866 when excavation began for Harmony Mills, Mill #3, (often referred to as Mastodon Mill) on Mohawk Street. Workmen uncovered the bones of a mastodon embedded in bowl-shaped depressions of bedrock. These cavities formed by the ancient beating and grinding action of falling water, which displaced rocks at the base of the Cohoes Falls. There, under a solidified mass of peat, vegetative debris, twigs, beaver-gnawed wood, and tree limbs embedded in loam, rested the bones of a male mastodon, sixty feet down.

The *Cohoes Cataract Newspaper* reported:

"Those who during the present generation have trod the earth of Cohoes have never taken onto their wildest imaginings the strange things concealed beneath the surface. But the late excavations made by the Harmony Company have brought to light the fact that a huge mastodon once dwelt where our village now stands . . ."

Mammoths (*Mammuthus primigenius*), also referred to as Woolly Mammoths, shared a similar structure to the mastodon, but grew larger. The daunting creature with its long, dense hair, large ears, lengthy trunks and tusks (incisors)—the longest of which measured 17 feet—stood at a height of over 15 feet. Their powerful tusks came in handy as protection and as digging instruments in their search for food. These herbivores (plant and grass eaters) possessed flat chewing teeth. They inhabited grassy plain regions.

Gone!

Success in sustaining life, for all species, including man, is about survival of the fittest. In the case of Ice Age mammals, a plethora of theories and varying schools of thought exist on the ultimate cause of their extinction. Did climate and geographical change following the glacier melt down cause this eradication? Was it the resulting diminished availability of their usual prey? Or, did human hunters massacre them, entirely? Scientists have probed a multitude of factors as contributing causes. The current agreed upon theory is the extinction resulted as a combination of ecological and climate changes in addition to the introduction of man, as hunter.[3]

BAM!

Most people are more familiar with the disappearance of dinosaurs than they are about the extinction of Ice Age mammals. One theory proposes a meteor collision caused the dinosaur extinction, by precipitating a large scale climate change. Could a similar event also be applied to the extinction of Ice Age mammals?

The theory asserts a giant asteroid or comet collided with Earth, striking just off the coast of the Yucatan peninsula 65 million years ago. Researchers, who believe dinosaur extinction quickly followed this event, also suggest the effects of this collision caused other forms of life to perish.

The impact created dense clouds of dust that blocked the sun's rays, causing a darkening of the atmosphere and an intense chilling of temperatures on planet Earth. This prompted the demise of most plants and, in turn, many animal species. When the dust settled, greenhouse gases drastically propelled temperatures upward. According to this theory, the extreme difference between frigid and sweltering temperatures caused the extinction of the dinosaurs, as well as up to 70% of all vegetation and other animals living at the time.[4]

How Did Their World Change?

"Yummo! A dandelion. Must be the last of the season."
~ Sid the Sloth

Modern science continues to study and report its findings as to how Ice Age mammals became extinct. But how did the *animals* experience these factors?

Most important, their normal diets and eating habits changed dramatically, resulting in a negative impact on their life spans. Scientists believe the development of greenhouse gases after the meteor collision sent temperatures upward; under optimum atmospheric changes this might have seemed like a good thing. However, the kind and amount of vegetation that existed before never returned to its former state nor grew in the same locations. After global warming, "old" ecosystems never re-established themselves to the same extent as before the warming.

At what is called the Last Glacial Maximum (25,000 – 15,000 years ago), the coldest and driest time of the Ice Age, a major loss of plant diversity took place and animals barely survived. The deprivation most affected mammoths and sloths. This new vegetation growth (tree leaves, grasses and plants) did not provide the same nutritional value of former food sources and lacked the bounty in normal grazing locations.

In regions of the global Northern Hemisphere, erroneous reports (according to some researchers) described the terrain as being "dominated by a grass steppe", when, in fact, the protein-rich *forbs*—broad-leaved herbs other than grass, found in fields, prairies or meadows—populated the landscape. As the Ice Age abated, *forbs* became increasingly rare, along with animals that relied upon them for survival.

Map depicts earth as it looked during the Ice Age, 14000 years B.C.E.

Enough to Eat . . . But Not With Bad Teeth

The saber-toothed tiger did not die of starvation or become extinct for lack of prey, according to some researchers. Its eventual demise came about due to poorly adapted dental features—those long, knife-point canines.

Larisa DeSantis, a vertebrate paleontologist at Vanderbilt University, Nashville, proposes,

> "In the case of the great cats, we expect that it would have been difficult for them to find prey, especially if they had to compete with humans. We know that when food becomes scarce, carnivores like the great cats tend to consume more of the carcasses they kill. If they spent more time chomping on bones, it should cause detectable changes in the wear patterns on their teeth."

After analyzing wear patterns on the fossilized teeth of saber-toothed tigers and big cats of comparable size and diet—African lions, cheetahs, dire wolves and coyotes—DeSantis concluded dental damage occurred more often while capturing prey instead of feeding on carcasses.

Climate Change

Smilodon fed on the enormous mammoths and four-ton, giant ground sloths. The massive size difference of this ancient cat and its prey compared to contemporary predators, could explain why the cat suffered more broken, hence unusable, teeth. Larger teeth break are more brittle than smaller teeth and carnivores like the saber-toothed tiger were more likely to break teeth taking down larger prey. A fox's canines can support more than 7 times their weight before breaking; a lion's canines can support 4 times their weight, but the curved teeth of the saber-tooth tiger could only support twice the weight of its prey.

One fact is certain: mammoths, mastodons, saber-toothed tigers, and giant ground sloths disappeared around 12,000 years ago, just as Earth began to warm and humans began to appear.[5]

Home Sweet Home: Remnants of the Past in New York State

The Ice Age ended in New York just about 8,000 years ago. In geologic time, these geographic events and creation of land formations are closer in time to us than they appear. Ice glaciers of one to two miles thick covered the majority of the state, except for a small section in southwestern New York known as the Salamanca Re-entrant. The majority of New York State existed under water between 500 and 300 million years ago.

The process of *glaciations* (how glaciers carved out and changed land by their movement) in New York State produced fascinating topographical phenomena. The majestic mountainous regions like the Adirondacks, U-shaped valleys in the Finger Lakes region, deep erosion in the Hudson River fjord, Tides on the Hudson near Albany, and the water basins which formed the Great Lakes and numerous smaller lakes across New York State, are a few examples of these natural formations.

The Adirondack region is, perhaps, one of the most unique in the state, as it contains some of the oldest rocks—over one-billion years old—in the entire country. In recent years minor earthquakes have been recorded in the Adirondacks, causing an *uplift* of the mountainous terrain in the Northeastern part of the state. This "rise" continues to produce younger mountain formations in the ancient, metamorphic rock of the Adirondack range.

When the glaciers receded, they left in their wake deposits of rocks and dirt, which filled the valleys with rich, fertile soil. These deposits—called *moraines*—characterized Central New York (the Finger Lakes), the Southern tier of the state and most notably, Long Island. These moraine deposits ranged from powdery silt to large rocks and boulders, which remained long after glaciers receded and had the awesome effect of diverting the courses of rivers, such as the Genesee and the Allegheny. The resulting water streams of melting glaciers contributed to forming the topography of New York State, as they cascaded down the Mohawk Valley, deepened the valley at Little Falls, and breached a wide, low-level divide that would become the path of the Erie Canal.[6]

New York City: A Geologic Oddity

New York City literally washed into place by glacial activity and its by-products: moraines, lakes and ponds, streams and valleys, kettle holes (depressions made from detached slabs of glacial ice), and peat bogs. Six-thousand years ago rising sea waters breached the morainal dam at what is now the Verrazano Narrows (the entrance to New York Harbor, connecting Brooklyn and Staten Island). Waters of the Hudson Lake burst into the present-day channel of the Hudson River and continued to rise, settling at the level it maintains today. When the watery pummeling and battering ceased, an archipelago, called New York City, emerged.

...With Its Ups and Downs

From a geological perspective, New York City displays a different natural history than other parts of the state with its abundance of igneous and metamorphic rock. Geologists attribute this to a "violent history of volcanism and colliding tectonic plates". A tectonic plate is a massive, irregularly shaped slab of solid rock. At one time, mountains thousands of feet high defined New York City's terrain. The towering skyscrapers that define the city's skyline today are anchored in hard, ancient metamorphic rock.[7]

The First Humans to Arrive

Just when we think the debate over animal extinction has resolved, there's another pivotal question afoot: who, in fact, were the first documented humans

Climate Change

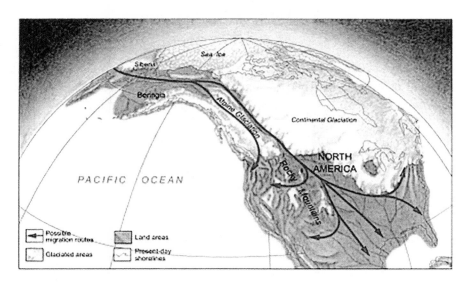

The Clovis people are believed to have migrated across the Bering Land Bridge to the Americas.

to arrive and where did they come from?

Some theories support the argument that the first peoples—Native Americans, as we know them—originated in Northeast Asia. They entered the Americas by one of two or *both* routes: the watercraft route along the Northwest Coast of North America, or by a pedestrian land route across the Bering Land Bridge (known as Beringia), as the continental route (through what is now the state of Alaska), then south through central-western Canada, beginning 16,300 years ago. Countering opinions suggest human migration emerged from the *Southern* and/or European hemispheres before surfacing in the Americas.

The theory that humans first entered America via a land route in the high Northern latitudes still holds as the prevailing belief. This concept is, in fact, deeply supported by scientific research. It is believed these peoples adapted to harsh, frigid temperatures and, indeed, hunted Ice Age mammals, as they crossed the Land Bridge into Alaska then moved south into central-western Canada, and finally, into more southern areas of North and South America.[8]

The "Clovis First"

The migration of the *Clovis* people into parts of North America supports the most widely-recognized archaeological theory they were the first inhabitants of the Americas. The Clovis people, also known as "Clovis First", are considered to be the ancestors of the most primal, indigenous culture of New York.[9]

They were the first New Yorkers.

Chapter 2

The First Peoples

Their name comes from the place where paleoanthropologists first found their artifacts in the 1920s: Clovis, New Mexico. The Clovis culture is estimated to have appeared at the end of the last glacial period, approximately 11,000 RCYBP years ago (uncalibrated Radiocarbon Years before Present). Distinctive bone and ivory tools, manufactured into what were termed "Clovis points", are believed to have been created and utilized between 13,200 to 12,900 calendar years ago. [1]

The Clovis People were primarily big game hunters thought by some to have caused the extinction of large bodied animals.

The Clovis became the first big game hunters on the North American continent, and as such, is often blamed for the general disappearance of the animals they hunted: mastodons, horses, camels, sloths, wolves, tapirs, and bears. As a hunting culture, they lived a nomadic existence and their campsites could be found in wide distribution. It is estimated they arrived in Western New York State between 8,000 to 9,000 years ago. [2]

The Lamoka and the Hopewell Indians

The Lamoka Culture followed the remnants of Clovis inhabitation in New York State. "Lamoka" is a native word meaning "Mud Lake". The Lamokas lived on or near bodies of water between Lamoka and Waneta lakes in what is now the town of Tyrone in Schuyler County, New York. The earliest bones from this culture date back 3000 years. The Lamokas hunted and fished, using both bone and stone tools honed into projectile points and polished, multi-faceted stone adzes (ax –like implements with arched blades). Such historical markers identify the Tyrone site as the oldest prehistoric, active village, formed just 1,000 years ago, in New York State.[3]

The Lamokas primarily made their homes in caves, but research by New York State Archaeologist, Dr. William Ritchie, indicates they may have also lived in round, above-ground structures. Their diet consisted of deer, turkey, fish, and acorns. Women cooked in basin-shaped hearths with stone slab covers. Their locations were conducive to travel by foot, by horse, or by canoe along the many streams of what would emerge as the Susquehanna system.[4]

The Hopewell Indians succeeded the Lamokas around 300 A.D. Considered a nebulous culture of sorts, history cannot concretely pin down their original travels and settlements. Two theories exist. The first is these people lived near Lake Erie, and then expanded west or south. The second theory is they first lived near Lake Superior, then expanded east and south. A third possibility is they didn't move at all, but invited other budding cultures to join their existing locations.[5]

Like the Lamokas, the Hopewell founded their settlements along river banks and they traveled mostly by canoe. They were large-scale farmers, cultivating an ecosystem, mainly consisting of squash, sunflower seeds, wild rice, and grasses. Some Hopewell also hunted deer, waterfowl, beaver, duck, buffalo, elk, rodents, and fish. They also excelled in copper and stone carvings and grew and smoked tobacco.

The Hopewell are recognized as master builders of earth mound complexes, from very rudimentary storage enclosures to elaborate burial structures. The buildings often covered several acres. Depending on the social stature of a deceased person, burials could be accompanied by a wealth of decorative and valuable goods, made of "exotic" natural materials and artifacts covered in red ochre, sheets of copper, mica, obsidian, polished stones, painted

The First Peoples

fabrics, beads, figurines, pottery bowls, animal jaws, and teeth.[6]

The Hopewell culture also traded in a sophisticated exchange network, where both raw and exotic materials passed among neighboring groups and over vast areas of northern and middle-America. By 400 A.D., however, this thriving culture virtually disappeared.

The Lenapes of Manhattan Island

The Lenape Indians (later known as the Delaware Indians) occupied New York City, or what they called Manahatta ("hilly island"), long before the arrival of Europeans in the mid-1500s. The body of water off the coast of Lower Manhattan is an estuary, where saltwater from the Atlantic Ocean mixes with freshwater from the Hudson River. The Lenape called it "Shatemuc", meaning "the river that flows both ways". This apt name perfectly describes the Hudson's alternating north-to-south flow in counterpoint with the tides of the Atlantic.[7]

The general physical geography of Lenape territories was vast, encompassing the Delaware River watershed, southeastern Pennsylvania, New Jersey, Western Long Island, and the Lower Hudson Valley communities along the river from Albany and Troy; and southward to Yonkers and Westchester County.[8]

The Lenapes and the Iroquois Nation were long standing opposition.

The Iroquois: Haudenosaunee ("People of the Longhouse") or the Six Nations

Over the next 1,000 years, the area south of the Saint Lawrence River became densely settled by the Iroquois Indians. Their choice of location would prove to be extremely profitable. The St. Lawrence River begins at the mouth of the Ontario River in Canada, courses through the Canadian provinces of Quebec and Ontario and finally forms part of the international boundary between Ontario and New York State. This mighty river would be known as the bustling Saint Lawrence Seaway; a tremendous boon to trade and future commerce.

The completion of the Erie Canal (1825), would be viewed by members of the Iroquois Nation as a detriment to its survival. The canal would be built around and through the lands occupied by its natives, thus displacing resident tribes along its path —from New York City's Hudson River to upstate New

York and Lake Erie; and eventually to the Great Lakes, and the Ohio and Mississippi River systems by additional canals.

The Erie Canal would not only connect the east to the expanding West and North, but it would also increase a burgeoning trade industry and serve as reliable transportation for settlers who sought to acquire tribal lands. State and federal policies called for "Indian removal" from portions of New York and neighboring states. Native peoples would be relocated to other reservations in comparatively isolated parts of those states and distant territories in the American Midwest. Ironically, it would be the Erie Canal that transported Oneida natives to Canada, Wisconsin, and to Kansas territories.[9]

Conflict Within: The Iroquois Confederacy is born

As the native Iroquois population grew, conflicts arose within its ranks. An aggressive people the Iroquois engendered inter-tribal conflict and warfare among themselves and Algonquian rival tribes.

Incessant bickering over geographic rule and participating in war-like activities became major concerns for the Mohawk prophet and spiritual leader, Deganawida ("The Great Peacemaker") and his disciple, Chief Hiawatha, of the Onondaga tribe. These leaders feared that this kind of dissension would weaken the Iroquois Nation. Jikohnsaseh (the Peace Mother), a wise woman of a neutral Lake Erie tribe, joined the spiritual leaders. Together, they established the Great Law of Peace or the Iroquois Confederacy and its member tribes accepted the constitution.

The Iroquois Confederacy emerged as a cultural and political union of Native American tribes residing in New York State. They included the Mohawk ("People of the Flint"), the Oneida ("People of the Upright Stone"), the Onondaga ("People of the Hills"), the Cayuga ("People of the Great Swamp"), and the Seneca ("People of the Great Hill"). A sixth tribe, the Tuscarora ("Shirt-Wearing People"), joined in 1722 as non-voting members after the five original tribes united between 1450 and 1600.[10]

The objectives of a unified Iroquois Nation included:

- The elimination of inter-tribal warfare.
- The creation of peace and strength.
- The creation of a forceful tribe.

The First Peoples

- The safeguarding and defense of existing Iroquois territories against outside invasion.
- The expansion of Iroquois territories.
- The establishment of a democratic government with representatives from each member tribe to ensure equity and fairness.
- Cessation of the custom of cannibalism.

The Constitution of the Iroquois Confederacy

The Constitution of the Iroquois Confederacy contained 117 Articles outlining its organization, how it functioned, and other items, such as:

- The Role of the Great Council, Council Membership, Eligibility and Resignation, Candidates, Election of Pine Tree Chiefs.
- The Election of the Chiefs, the Duties and Rights of War Chiefs, Women, Clans, and Consanguinity (a blood relationship by descent from the same ancestor; not by marriage or affinity).
- Official Symbolism, Wampum, Laws of Adoption.
- Laws of Emigration, Rights of Foreign Nations, Rights and Powers of War, Treason or Secession of a Nation.
- The Protection of Religious Ceremonies, Protection of the House (the Meeting Longhouse,) and Funeral Addresses.[11]

The Significance of the Longhouse

Deganawida and Hiawatha designated the Longhouse as a symbol of the union of member tribes, of the culture and traditions of the Iroquois people, and how their territory should be shared. The three largest tribes decided who would rule over land divisions.

The Mohawk were "Keepers of the Eastern Door"; the Seneca (the largest tribe of the Iroquois Nation) became "Keepers of the Western Door" and the Onondaga were the "Keepers of the Central Council Fire and Wampum".* This tribe's main village served as the group's meeting place.

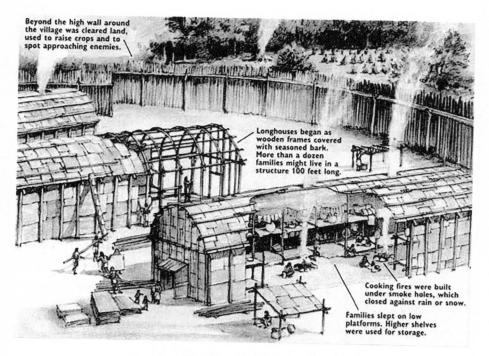

Beyond the high wall around the village was cleared land, used to raise crops and to spot approaching enemies.

Longhouses began as wooden frames covered with seasoned bark. More than a dozen families might live in a structure 100 feet long.

Cooking fires were built under smoke holes, which closed against rain or snow.

Families slept on low platforms. Higher shelves were used for storage.

The Great Council

The Great Council consisted of clan and village chiefs, chosen by The Great Peacemaker (Deganawida), to govern the confederacy. This group comprised an assembly of 50 sachems. The Iroquois Constitution insisted upon unanimous agreement within the Council of Chiefs before any propositions could be carried out. It also gave significant power to clan mothers (matriarchs or respected female leaders), who often selected the chiefs. This body of 50 voting members included 14 from the Onondaga, 10 from the Cayuga, 9 from the Mohawk, 8 from the Seneca, and 9 from the Oneida.[12]

A Sophisticated Political System

The Iroquois Confederacy included a bicameral (two-house) legislature, much like the United States Congress and the British Parliament. The Iroquois document strongly influenced the writers of the American Constitution. The Iroquois Society served as an example of political and military prowess, an adaptive, interactive lifestyle, and a supporter of the elevated role of women.

The Iroquois were the largest and most relentless threat to European settlements. Throughout their history of conquest and ensuing land treaties, their durable legacy remains. Benjamin Franklin greatly admired the Iroquois.[13]

Highlights of Iroquois Life

- The Iroquois lived in villages populated with longhouses.* These large, hundred-foot-long, wood-frame buildings were covered with roofs made of elm tree bark and animal skins hung over them as added insulation and covering. A hole cut in the roof allowed smoke to escape. Entire clans (multiple families) of up to 60 people could live in one longhouse, proving the Iroquois rule that all would live peacefully under one roof.

- Known as the "Sustainers of Life," the Iroquois considered corn, beans and squash to be special gifts from the Creator. They believed the viability of each crop to be protected by one of the Three Sister Spirits, which must never be separated; but planted together, consumed together and celebrated together.

- The Iroquois were skilled artisans, clever woodworkers, and the original craftsmen of the Lacrosse stick, which is credited to the Cayuga tribe. By wetting and steaming strips of wood, they bent them to create curved tools and weapons, as well as sticks to use in an early game of Lacrosse. Tribe members played the game as a method of settling inter-tribal disputes without violence. Today, Iroquois artisans make Lacrosse Sticks using the same techniques as their ancestors.

- Mohawk men were fierce warriors who first sported the famous "Mohawk haircut"—completely shaven heads, except for a scalp lock or plume of hair down the center of the head. In battle, they sometimes added feathers or brightly dyed animal fur to the center strip.

- The Iroquois had no writing system. They communicated their history through their prolific language. Sacred beads and shells called wampum were attached to belts to record special events. The Iroquois Confederacy recorded "minutes" of their meetings on the Hiawatha Wampum Belt, which held symbols of each of the five original tribes.

- Polly Cooper, an Oneida woman, taught the soldiers of George Washington's Continental Army how to prepare life-saving corn. Accepting no payment for her services, she eventually accepted a gift bonnet and shawl from Martha Washington. The shawl is still in existence today.

- The Sullivan Expedition (1779) —a military campaign employing 6,200 troops, was designed to unseat the Iroquois Confederacy, thus ending its attacks on the Continental Army and its New York militias. The siege destroyed approximately 50 Cayuga villages along with its lands and crops. At the end of the Revolutionary War, the Cayuga tribe was the only Haudenosaunee tribe without a land reservation.

- The Onondaga, known as "Keepers of the Fire", lived primarily near Syracuse, NY. Modern day chiefs still meet there.

- Known for migrating with the seasons, the Tuscarora (originally a coastal plain tribe in North Carolina), lived in round, squat houses with domed roofs in the summer, and each winter they migrated closer to friendly tribes and erected similar houses with fire pits. Known as "hemp gatherers", these people used the wild plant to insulate their houses. Ultimately, colonists defeated the Tuscarora in the Tuscarora War. They brought disease to tribal populations, seized Indian land, and sold their women and children into slavery. The Tuscarora became the first native people to be dispossessed of their land during colonization, and walked north to New York in the early eighteenth century to join the League of the Iroquois or the Six Nations.[14]

The First Peoples

People of Interest
Handsome Lake: "The Good Word" (Gaihwiyo)

The Seneca religious leader of the Iroquois people, Handsome Lake, played a major role in reviving, or sterilizing, traditional religion among the Haudenosaunee. He was also half-brother to Cornplanter, a Seneca war chief. Handsome Lake lived in the village of Canawaugus, (now, the Town of Caledonia) located on the Genesee River near present-day Avon, New York.

After what is described as "a period of illness" due to many years of excessive alcohol consumption, Handsome Lake experienced "visions". In them, three spiritual messengers warned him about the dangers associated with alcohol; they also told him that witches were creating chaos within his tribe and that the persons guilty of witchcraft must repent and confess.

He became obsessed with witch hunting and with seeking confessions from those whom he only suspected of witchcraft. He killed those who refused to confess. His own people turned against him for his over-zealous mission. As a result, he stopped his futile witch hunt and briefly assumed a less prominent leadership role.

Shortly after his first vision, he stopped drinking alcohol and began a religious movement which combined traditional Iroquois beliefs with elements of Christianity, primarily from those of the Quakers. His message created a moral system referred to as the Code of Handsome Lake, or the Good Word (Gaihwiyo), the "new religion". The Code outlawed drunkenness, witchcraft, sexual promiscuity, wife beating, and quarreling.

In 1794 he signed the Pickering Treaty with the support of the six Iroquois Nation tribes. The treaty established peace and friendship between the United States and the Iroquois Nation, securing Haudenosaunee land rights in the state of New York.

Cornplanter: Seneca War Chief and Diplomat

Born John Abeel (1752–1836) in Canawaugus —the son of a Seneca mother and Dutch father (Johannes Abeel), and half-brother to Handsome Lake— Cornplanter (known by his farming skill) was a Seneca War Chief and respected diplomat.

As a warrior Chief, Cornplanter fought in both the French and Indian

War and the American Revolutionary War, despite the urgings of both American and British forces to remain neutral. In addition to the Seneca, three other Iroquois nations also became allies of the British: the Mohawk, the Onondaga and the Cayuga. After the Revolutionary War ended, Cornplanter led negotiations with the United States as a signatory of the Treaty of Fort Stanwix (1784); one of numerous treaties regarding Indian land ownership.

Chief Red Jacket: A Man of Conviction

Red Jacket negotiated with the American Government to secure lands for his people. He signed the Treaty of Canandaigua.

Chief Red Jacket (c. 1758-1838) was a Seneca chief and an impressive orator. Reports of his birthplace vary, but it is believed his father may have been a Cayuga. He gained his colorful name from the red coat the British gave him when he worked as their messenger. He was a relatively unremarkable, if not a somewhat cowardly warrior.

He was, however, a respected speaker, especially when proudly espousing Seneca values. He exerted strong influence at Buffalo Creek which remained the most populous Seneca reservation until its sale in 1838, after his death. He played a prominent role in grievance negotiations between his people and the new American republic, heading a delegation of 50 to Philadelphia, the US government seat in 1792. At this meeting, George Washington presented Red Jacket with a large, silver peace medal.

Red Jacket's influence was not without challenge. In 1801, Handsome Lake accused Red Jacket of practicing witchcraft. Red Jacket's eloquent defense of his personal conduct completely cleared him of the charge.

Cornplanter, Handsome Lake and Red Jacket would each go on to play pivotal roles in the social, religious, and the political transformation of New York; but, ultimately, they could not prevent the loss of their lands and the building of a great waterway that would change American life.

Part Two
THE EMPIRE STATE

Chapter 3
Discovery

L ike the first native inhabitants of the New World, European explorers set out to stake claim. They braved the elements, learned to tackle unfamiliar tasks to survive, and, in the process, encountered new things—and new people—for the first time.

Brave and Willing: Giovanni da Verrazzano (1485–1528) and Jacques Cartier (1491-1557)

When Giovanni da Verrazzano sailed into New York Harbor—at the mouth of the Hudson River, its Narrows, and their proximity to what would later become Staten Island—it is conjectured the French explorer, Jacques Cartier, accompanied him. He may have also joined Verrazzano on a few prior expeditions to the New World.

In 1524, King Francis I of France commissioned Verrazzano to sail to the Atlantic coast of North America. His chosen route resulted in trips between New Brunswick (Canada), Narragansett Bay (Rhode Island), New York Bay, and south to the Florida coast. When his flagship vessel, La Dauphine, reached the areas surrounding Cape Fear and the Pamlico Sound lagoon off the coast of North Carolina, he mistakenly believed he had found access to the Pacific Ocean and to China.[1]

Somehow, he didn't take note of the entrances to Chesapeake Bay or to the mouth of the Delaware River. Even if he had, these waterways would not provide an express lane to the Pacific Ocean. Many maps of the North American continent contained errors such as this, Canada, for example, was labeled "West".

Sailing northwards, Verrazzano unwittingly made his historic entrance into the Hudson River or New York Harbor, which he perceived to be a "large lake". Here, he encountered and communicated with the Lenape people. It is believed that he generally preferred to anchor at sea and not travel inland. On this trip, however, he and some crewmen rowed ashore in a small boat. The Lenape people welcomed them, providing food and gifts. From there, he sailed to Long Island and up to Narragansett Bay (Rhode Island) where he met the Wampanoag Indians.[2]

1528: A Gruesome Final Voyage

In 1528, Verrazzano again dispatched—for the last time—to the New World to explore the southern coastal waters of North America and their land regions; namely, those off the Florida coast, the Bahama Islands, and the Lesser Antilles. These islands, also known as the Caribbees, form the eastern boundary of the Caribbean Sea and the Atlantic Ocean.

The intrepid explorer anchored his ship at sea and, again, rowed a small boat to the shore of what he believed to be the island of Guadalupe, among the Lesser Antilles. This proved to be a fatal decision, resulting in his gruesome death.

There, he encountered native peoples called the Carib. Over time, the word "carib" would morph into English as "cannibal", which aptly referred to the common Carib ritual of killing and eating their enemies. Reports stated Verrazzano succumbed to this ghastly fate.[3]

Jacques Cartier (1491-1557)

In 1534, King Francis I commissioned French navigator Jacques Cartier to sail the Grande Hermine into the northern coastal areas of the New World in search of gold, valuable spices, and a water passage from France to Asia. Two months into his voyage, Cartier came upon the St. Lawrence River in eastern Canada. It was not going to take him all the way to Asia; but he had, in fact, discovered an important waterway into the vast northern territory which would later facilitate French colonization.

Discovery

He continued up the river to what is now Prince Edward Island, where he first met with Chief Donnacona and friendly natives of the Iroquois Nation. This meeting went so well that the chief allowed his sons, Taignoagny and Domagaya, to join Cartier's crew and travel home with him to France on the condition that they return.

Cartier did return the following year with the young native men, who acted as guides, in tow. He sailed down river from his first location to the Iroquois villages of Stadacona, which would become Quebec, and Hochelaga, present day Montreal.[4]

Cartier was the first French explorer to document the name "Canada" for this French native colony, which he derived from the Iroquois word, "kanata", meaning "village". He also referred to the native inhabitants as "Canadiens".

The Iroquois told him of other rivers farther west that contained gold, silver, and copper. Before he could continue, a harsh winter set in making the swift river rapids impassable. He returned to France and reported to the king that "untold riches lay farther west and that a great river, said to be about 2,000 miles long, possibly led to Asia."[5]

Henry Hudson (c.1565-1611)

In 1609 English explorer, Henry Hudson, took a voyage to the New World, under the auspices of the Dutch East India Company. He unintentionally "discovered" the New York river that would bear his name. He had been commissioned to find an ice-free waterway or a northwest passage to Cathay (China). He failed on two previous attempts, sponsored by English merchants.

He was not the first European explorer to discover the river. Yet, when it comes to historical bragging rights, Verrazzano's previous achievement seems trumped by Hudson, who indeed traveled farther up into the river than its previous explorer. After traveling approximately 150 miles in a northerly direction, Hudson's vessel, the Half Moon, did not reach the Pacific, but it did come upon an area which would later become Albany, New York. [6]

Painting depicting Henry Hudson sailing into what later would become New York Harbor, September 3, 1609.

A Picture is Worth a Thousand Words

It is believed that Hudson's first steps onto New World soil occurred along the coast of Staten Island. It is likely that this is when his first meeting with native inhabitants—who had never seen a white man—also took place. It is reported that the Indians described Hudson as wearing "a red coat with glittering gold lace". He described crude native dress as that made of deer and other animal skins. He sailed up river and anchored along the Narrows that would become the site of the Verrazano-Narrows Bridge.

He proceeded north to Indian Point in the Catskill Mountains and invited natives aboard the Half Moon for the first time. There he traded steel knives, hatchets, and beads for native corn, bread, and oysters. The crew correctly judged the plethora of animal fur as a potentially profitable commodity for trade. This historic trip would lay the foundation for Dutch colonization in the New World.

Hudson's fourth trip to the New World in 1611 ended in tragedy. After living through a frigid winter with his crew on the shores of James Bay, south of Hudson Bay in Canada, Hudson insisted on heading west. His weary and exhausted crew mutinied, physically casting Hudson and seven other men over the side of the ship. Those remaining sailed back to England where they were hanged.[7]

Discovery

New Netherland - The First Dutch Settlement in New York (1624)

Between 1609 and 1664 the Netherlands, exclusively, held land in the Hudson River Valley. Its colonies collectively established a network of trading posts, towns, and forts under the name of New Netherland. The settlers called the northernmost site Fort Orange which is present day Albany. They named the New York City area New Amsterdam, and Wiltwyck, the third largest of this settlement, is Kingston, New York, today.

In an effort to boost colonization in its New World locale, the Dutch Parliament hired the West India Company, a joint stock company, to oversee all Dutch ventures in the Western Hemisphere. In 1624, 30 Dutch families arrived in what is now New York City. These first settlers had no interest in cultivating the land, but planned to take advantage of the lucrative fur trade.

In 1626, Peter Minuit—a French-speaking Belgian—arrived at the settlement. The West India Company subsequently named him administrator (governor) of the Dutch colony. They instructed him to settle the purchase of Manhattan Island with its Indian inhabitants.

His historic purchase of Manhattan Island from the Lenape Indians for

Peter Minuit (1585-1638), generally credited with orchestrating the purchase of Manhattan Island.

a mere 60 guilders—or 24 dollars—formally established Manhattan as New Amsterdam. The colony gradually grew as the company offered settlers generous land grants and trade opportunities, as they slowly moved further North along the Hudson River.

The Sale of Manhattan Island: A Bargain or a Blunder?

"Old Peter Minuit had nothing to lose when he bought the isle of Manhattan / For twenty-six dollars and a bottle of booze, and they threw in the Bronx and Staten / Pete thought he had the best of the bargain, but the poor red man just grinned / And he grunted "ugh!" for he knew poor Pete was skinned."

~ "Give It Back to the Indians"
Rodgers & Hart song, 1939

Beginning in grade school, we learn quite matter-of-factly that Peter Minuit (c.1580-85–1638) bought Manhattan Island from the Indians for $24. Sounds rather simple, doesn't it?

History proves this event to be far from simple and it had far reaching consequences. The problematic "sale" of Manhattan Island meant different things to the buyer(s) and the seller(s) and its documentation was flimsy, if not practically non-existent. In short, it readily opened the door for unrest between the Dutch and the native peoples in residence.

Native Americans revered the land and didn't think of it as property or a commodity that could be bought or sold. They fought among themselves over hunting or fishing areas, but had no concept of "right", or ownership, or exclusive use of pieces of land.

American law professor, G. Edward White, offers support for the probable Indian point of view regarding the Manhattan Island transaction. He claims the Indians believed they were "not relinquishing the island, but simply welcoming the Dutch as additional occupants... in a property rights system that was different from the Europeans'... (thus) allowing the Dutch hunting or use(r) rights on the island... while assuming continuing rights of their own".[8]

Discovery

An Urban Myth?

The Indians didn't sell Minuit some hot swamp land in Florida. Could the sale of Manhattan Island be the first urban myth? What did this sale mean? To date, no deed or land transfer has ever been found, nor a formal title or bill of sale to prove the legality of the transaction.[9]

But, there is a letter, dated November 5, 1626, locked away in the Dutch National Archives in the Hague, Netherlands, which refers to the "sale of the Manhattes", written by Dutch merchant, Pieter Schagen. Contained in it is this information: "They have purchased the island of Manhattes from the savages for the value of 60 guilders." Minuit's name doesn't appear anywhere.

Critical details are sorely missing from this document; such as its date, the names of the buyer(s), the names of the seller(s); what type of payment they tendered, and so on. How could 60 guilders or $24 dollars worth of beads and trinkets be calculated? While it is believed that the Lenapes were the natives involved in the sale, the Manahatin, the Canarsie, the Shinnecock, and the Munsee native tribes also populated Lower Manhattan at the time. Which "savages" made the deal?

Here are copies of the original letter and its English translation. At best, it is vague and confusing. It reads like a post card or newsletter; not as a title, a bill, or document of ownership. Who is the "they" to which Schagen refers? Doesn't the cargo listed appear to be what the Indians might have traded for beads and trinkets? Some historians say that axes, iron kettles, and woolen clothing also comprised part of what the Dutch "paid", since the natives were shrewd bargainers and would not have settled for a pile of worthless trinkets and glass.

Translation
Recep. 7 November 1626
High and Mighty Lords,

Yesterday the ship the Arms of Amsterdam arrived here. It sailed from New Netherland out of the River Mauritius on the 23d of September. They report that our people are in good spirit and live in peace. The women also have borne some children there. They have purchased the Island of Manhattes from the savages for the value of 60 guilders. It is

11,000 morgens in size. They had all their grain sowed by the middle of May, and reaped by the middle of August. They sent samples of these summer grains: wheat, rye, barley, oats, buckwheat, canary seed, beans and flax.

The cargo of the aforesaid ship is:

7246 Beaver skins
178½ Otter skins
675 Otter skins
48 Mink skins
36 Lynx skins
33 Minks
34 Muskrat skins
many oak timbers and nut wood.

Herewith, High and Mighty Lords, be commended to the mercy of the Almighty,

In Amsterdam, the 5th of November anno 1626.

Your High and Mightinesses' obedient

(Signed, 'P. Schaghen')

Rather than establishing any sort of equitable land or trade agreement, the sale of Manhattan Island gave determined governments and impatient colonists the green light to occupy, if not seize as their own, physical geography inhabited by Native Americans; their homes, their goods and, sadly, their well-being.

War!

By 1639, the prickly coexistence of Native Americans and Dutch colonists became a boiling kettle waiting to explode; and when it did, something as benign as a ripe peach is thought to have sparked a series of brutal attacks, known as the Peach Tree Wars of 1655.[10]

Discovery

Seeds

In 1631, the Dutch West India Company suspended Peter Minuit from his post as governor of New Netherland. Possible reasons for his dismissal may have involved corrupt practices which allowed patroons (landholders with manorial rights to large land tracts in New Netherland) to engage in illegal fur trading against the interests and orders of the Dutch West India Company.

Yet, in 1638 Minuit returned to the New World. This time, the Swedish West India Company hired him to establish a colony in America, which he named "New Sweden". He did this after he "purchased" the land from the Susquehannock Indians who remained leery of Minuit and his association with the Dutch and with their native rivals, the Iroquois Confederation. In August of the same year, Minuit embarked on a trading mission to the Caribbean and died at sea during a tropical storm.

He founded New Sweden on the Delaware River, in what is now Wilmington, Delaware. The colony spread out over parts of the present day states of Delaware, New Jersey, and Pennsylvania. The Susquehannock people, also known by the English as the Conestoga, occupied this area. They lived near the Susquehanna River —from southern New York, through east and central Pennsylvania (west of the Pocono Mountains), and extended along the west bank of the Potomac River in Maryland to the north end of the Chesapeake Bay. Up to 20 smaller tribes made up the Susquehannock people who occupied villages all along the river. Settlers considered them to be the leading tribal power on the Eastern seaboard, remaining independent from other native nations through the 1600s.

The Susquehannock also predominately supplied furs and pelts to the New Sweden colony, which became a protectorate and tributary (a state that pays tribute to another state) of the Susquehannock nation.

"Big Belly" and Johan Risingh

Johan Björnsson Printz governed the New Sweden colony from 1643 to 1653. He was energetic, conscientious, and a big man, weighing 400 pounds. The Lenni Lenape people nicknamed him "Big Belly". Under his tenure, Swedish farmers easily dealt with the natives, establishing an atmosphere of kindness and fairness. Printz achieved amicable relations with English settlers and initiated trade with the Dutch colonies in New Netherland.

When New Sweden ran short of supplies from its mother country, Printz found himself unprepared and unable to prevent the English and Dutch from encroaching on the profitable beaver fur trade in the area. The new director general of New Netherland, Peter Stuyvesant became his nemesis. This put Printz in an impossible, pressured position and he returned to Sweden in 1654. Johan Classon Risingh immediately replaced him as governor.

This transition of power benefited both the Dutch and English, who had gone about creating a virtual monopoly of the fur trade. However, they still appeared to view New Sweden's key location on the Delaware River as a concern; more likely, as a threat to business and profits. The Dutch, in particular, became even more concerned when they discovered that the Swedish settlement had been situated just above the 42-degree parallel North, which marked the extent, or cut-off point, of the Dutch land claim in North America. In 1651, the Dutch relocated Fort Nassau, one of its larger forts, further south—just 6.5 miles downstream from the Swedish fort, Fort Christina, and renamed their new fort, Fort Casimir.

Too Close for Comfort

In 1654, on Trinity Sunday, Governor Johan Risingh took a proactive step to deter the Dutch from continuing to monopolize the fur trade and expel them from the Delaware Valley. He ordered an assault on Fort Casimir. The Dutch surrendered and again renamed their fort. This time, they chose the name Fort Trefaldighet or Fort Trinity.

Finally, the Swedes possessed their colony in its entirety. On June 21, 1654, the Indians met with the Swedish settlers to reaffirm their trading agreements and amicable relationship. Their peace was short lived.

Between September 11th and 15th of 1665, an armed squadron of Dutch ships, under the direction of Director-General Peter Stuyvesant, attacked and seized New Sweden.

The Susquehannock retaliated.

Dutch and Indian Wars (1641-1645)- a series of armed conflicts between the Dutch colony of New Netherland and the Algonquins.

The Attack

The Susquehannock stood in a dominant place, politically and militarily, allowing them to put together an army of warriors from multiple allied tribes. A band of 500-600 men arrived in New Amsterdam (Lower Manhattan), raided homes, farms, food supplies, and mostly, the sense of peace and prosperity Dutch residents had come to expect.

They crossed the North River (the southernmost part of the Hudson River in New York City/northeastern New Jersey) into Pavonia (Jersey City), Hoboken, and Staten Island, launching an attack that lasted 3 days. The natives killed one-hundred Dutch, captured 150, and took them hostage. They also attacked farms in Harlem (northern Manhattan) and the Bronx. Peter Stuyvesant was not in New Amsterdam at the time of the attacks, but quickly returned to the city. The Indians collected ransom, and left those settlers whose homes they had destroyed on the western shores of the river, to take temporary refuge in New Amsterdam.[11]

The Aftermath

The Dutch seemed to be at a loss as to why the Susquehannock attack took place, even as their troops attacked Swedish settlements on the Delaware River! The Swedish settlers had developed good trading relationships with the natives; relationships the Dutch seemed intent on destroying. The Susquehannock had come to view the Swedes as allies, whom they deemed worthy of protection.

The New Netherland colonists believed the attack was motivated by something else: a peach. They believed the Susquehannock retaliated for the murder of a young Indian woman who "stole" a single peach from the tree of a Dutch settler, who ran for his gun and shot her. The Peach Tree Wars became the last major Dutch-Indian hostility in the colony.

The French and Indian War (1754-1763): Was it George Washington's Fault?

The British and French colonies fought the French and Indian War or The Seven Years War. At the time, North America contained approximately 60,000 French settlers, compared to approximately 2 million British settlers. France and Great Britain militarily supported their own settlers. Each side— particularly the French—also enlisted the support of Native American allies. The war would be widespread, from Virginia to Nova Scotia.

Not surprisingly, war began over a land dispute in the expansive Ohio Valley, involving the Allegheny and Monongahela rivers (called the Forks of Ohio) and the site of the French fort, Fort Duquesne, in present-day Pittsburgh, Pennsylvania. The Ohio River connected to the Mississippi River, which provided critical access for the transport of goods produced in the area.

Message Delivered

Governor Robert Dinwiddie of Virginia sent a young, ambitious, 22-year-old Major George Washington to confront the French in the Ohio Valley, by delivering the message that the French were to leave the region and end their harassment of English settlers.

Washington left Williamsburg, Virginia, in October of 1753, accompanied by Jacob Van Braam, and Christopher Gist, an Ohio trader and guide. They

Discovery

arrived 2 months later in a raging snowstorm at Fort LeBoeuf, located on the shores of Lake Erie in Pennsylvania. Captain Jacques Legardeur de Saint-Pierre politely greeted them and wrote his succinct reply to Dinwiddie: "The French king's claim to the Ohio Valley is incontestable".

Washington and his party headed back to Virginia, traveling almost 900 miles in the hard winter of 1753, and arriving 2½ months later. The French refusal to vacate the Ohio River Valley personally concerned Washington, in addition to his half-brothers, Lawrence and Augustine Washington, Governor Robert Dinwiddie, George William Fairfax, and George Mason —all of whom held shares of the Ohio Company, established in 1749 to help settlers develop the Ohio Valley region.[12]

George Washington during the French-Indian War. It is generally not known that Washington lost most of his military engagements prior to the Revolutionary war.

Each shareholder had been granted between 200,000 to 300,000 acres of land between the Kanawha and Monongahela Rivers. The French presence there posed an economical threat to the longevity of their company.

For All the World to See

Shortly after his return to Virginia, Washington penned a detailed report, the Journal of Major George Washington, of his experiences and observations in the Ohio Valley. The report impressed Governor Dinwiddie was and he had it published in Williamsburg newspapers, other American publications, and those in London. Dinwiddie also included his letter to the French and Captain Jacques Legardeur de Saint-Pierre's reply on behalf of the King of France.

The Journal of Major George Washington not only helped to inform the American and British of the growing French threat in the Ohio Valley, it also gave bold celebrity status, on both sides of the Atlantic, to the young American major.

The French remained resolute and defiant. In March of 1754, Dinwiddie promoted Washington to Lieutenant Colonel and ordered him and a Virginia militia of 160 men back to Ohio. He ordered Washington to, "Act on the defensive... (but) make prisoners of or kill and destroy those who resist British control of the region."

A History Making Skirmish: The Battle of Jumonville Glen

The French responded to Washington's presence by demanding an English withdrawal from the region and rounded up a force of French soldiers under the command of Ensign Joseph Coulon de Villers de Jumonville. They proceeded to camp close to Washington's forces in a rocky ravine called Great Meadows, in what is now Fayette County, Pennsylvania.

After leading a party of approximately 40 soldiers on an all-night march, along with Seneca chief, Tanacharison and 12 native warriors, Washington stealthily approached the French camp at dawn on May 28, 1754. When the French spotted his militia and fired upon them, Washington's men returned a surprise attack which overthrew the enemy. They killed thirteen French soldiers and Ensign Jumonville.

Naturally, each side claimed the other fired first. What could not be disputed was that this foray sparked a war that changed the course of history. From an international perspective, no conflict existed between France and Great Britain at the time this event occurred. They ruled their colonial settlements from afar. However, this clash—the Battle of Jumonville Glen—would forever be known as the beginning of the French and Indian War.

Colonial Reaction to the War: The Albany Congress
(June 19 to July 11, 1754)

In the early stages of the French and Indian War, the Albany Congress convened in Albany, New York. This marked the first time colonial representatives met to discuss the formation of a formal union. Legislative representatives from the northern seven of the 13 British colonies: Connecticut, Maryland, Massachusetts, New Hampshire, New York, Pennsylvania and Rhode Island attended this conference.

Delegates did not create an American union at this session, but formed collective plans which would improve and solidify trade relations with native tribes via a possible treaty with the Mohawk and/or with other major tribes of the Iroquois Nation. They also concerned themselves with formulating better defensive measures against the threat of French advances from Canada.

The meeting brought the colonists together in a unifying way that would influence their future confederation in the Revolutionary War.

The End of the War

Most colonial battles in North America ended in 1760 with one important exception: the French seizure of St. John's—the capital and largest city in Newfoundland, Canada. When British General Amherst heard of this surprise action, he dispatched forces in return, and regained control of Newfoundland after the Battle of Signal Hill in September of 1762. It proved to be the last battle of the French and Indian War.

Great Britain, France (and Spain) signed the Treaty of Paris on February 10, 1763 which brought an official end to the French and Indian War and recognized Britain's victories during the seven-year span.[13]

France and Spain recorded the Treaty of Fountainbleu (1762) as a "secret" agreement between the two countries after the Battle of Signal Hill. King Louis XV of France ceded "the country known as Louisiana" to Spain. This agreement covered all of Louisiana, from the Mississippi River Valley to the Appalachians and the Rockies. The other parties had no knowledge of the existence of this treaty even during the negotiation and signing of the Treaty of Paris.[14]

King George III issued the Royal Proclamation of 1763 following Great Britain's acquisition of French territory in North America at the end of the French and Indian War. Many saw this as a conciliatory gesture by Great Britain toward Ottawa chief, Pontiac, who had united many tribes in the Ohio Valley against the British in their efforts to seize tribal lands. Pontiac's Rebellion initiated a series of raids on British forts and American settlements. The British eventually quashed the rebellion and created this proclamation, forbidding American colonists to settle on Native American territory unless native rights to the land had first been obtained by purchase or treaty.

The Psychic Highway

The Revolutionary War (1775-1783)

Before the French and Indian War, Britain bowed out of the affairs of the colonies, leaving them "free" to create governing rules to match their new classification as Americans. As such, they established representative legislatures and democratic town meetings, implementing local judiciaries and trials by jury in which defendants were assumed innocent until proven guilty.

The colonists thrived with a sense of freedom and the ability to prosper in the New World. During this time, they enjoyed what is known as a period of "salutary neglect": the unofficial, long-term British policy of avoiding strict enforcement of parliamentary laws meant to keep American colonies obedient to England.

After the French and Indian War, however, Britain ended this policy and began placing larger tax burdens and tighter regulations upon the colonies to replenish the financial deficit incurred in the war. Britain forbid Americans to circulate local printed currencies; forced them to comply with restrictive trade and shipping polices, and ordered colonists to house British troops, among other stipulations. Those failing to comply with the rules faced a British judge without a jury.[15]

Americans regarded these demands—and those to come—as violations of their liberties. Their shock and outrage turned to indignation and provided the impetus for rebellion.

Following a series of protests over taxes in the 1760s and 1770s, the colonies united politically and militarily in opposition to the British government. The American Revolutionary War ensued.

The American Revolution had profound consequences. Never before had a body of colonists deemed their monarch and government incapable of governing a free people. On July 2, 1776 colonial congressmen voted to declare independence. A young lawyer from Virginia named Thomas Jefferson drafted the Declaration of Independence.

The United States of America was born.

Chapter 4
Closing the Circle

The original geographic territory occupied by the Seneca comprised of 4 principal villages situated in the westernmost part of New York State between Seneca Lake and the Genesee and Allegheny Rivers. By 1651, the Seneca ranks had substantially increased. One contributing factor included the hefty numbers of captives taken in earlier tribal wars. One of the 4 Seneca villages was actually populated entirely by captives. In addition, the Seneca also absorbed groups of Neutrals (members of the Neutral Confederacy of Iroquois- speaking, indigenous peoples from the northern shores of Lake Ontario and Lake Erie) and of the Erie tribe in 1656. (See Appendix A)

Consequently, the Seneca expanded further westward, acquiring land near the Niagara River and Lake Erie. They became an increasingly powerful force. More than a century later, their villages numbered 30. The Seneca held a prominent position in tribal wars waged by the Iroquois Confederacy, fighting natives to the north, west, and south of their territories to control trade. They also attempted to create alliances and "fill the places" of their fallen dead. In colonial wars, these fierce warriors allied with the British against the French and later, against the Americans near the close of the Revolutionary War.[1]

The French continued to expand westward which prolonged ongoing conflict among the trade activities of the Seneca. Between 1651 and 1653, the Seneca and all allied Iroquois tribes, except the Mohawk, actively harassed the French until 1653 when they signed a peace treaty. Peace was short lived.

In 1654, a member of an Erie tribe delegation visited a Seneca village and became involved in a quarrel with a Seneca resident and killed him. The Seneca retaliated by killing all 30 members of the Erie delegation. A series of brutal attacks and counter-attacks followed, escalating into a full-blown war between the Erie and the entire Iroquois Nation. Viewed by many as the main phase of the Beaver Wars (also known as the Iroquois-Huron War, among other similar titles) the event erased the Erie Nation in 1656.[2]

On a Wing and a Prayer:
The Seneca Make Contact with Early Europeans

As they exercised territorial control, the Seneca most preferred to encounter traders, rather than unknown people and French Jesuit missionaries. Yet, the peace treaty of 1653 opened the door for Fr. Pierre-Joseph-Marie Chaumonot (1611-1693), to visit them in 1656. He is credited with founding the first mission among the Seneca. Presumably, France (King Louis XIV) sent Catholic missionaries to North America as a means of retaining its presence in the New World. What better way to accomplish this than by evangelizing heathen populations with the word of God.[3]

Basque nobleman, Ignatius Loyola founded the Jesuits (also known as the Society of Jesus) in 1540. All missionaries who followed him adopted his message. Quite simply, his mission advised, "In all things, (to) love and serve". The Jesuits went about accomplishing this by addressing the qualities of faith, justice, and respect for divergent cultures and by opening dialogue with potential converts.

These scholarly educators quickly learned native languages, which they spoke to communicate with indigenous tribes. The Jesuits developed dictionaries, translated prayers and hymns, recited them when addressing large groups, and managed to preserve much of this history in written documents.

Jesuit priests had the ability to adapt missionary methods to existing local cultures, incorporating the belief systems of indigenous peoples to introduce and explain the tenets of Christianity. They hoped by communicating this way, native populations would accept and adapt to European values, thereby forming stable, ethical societies.[4]

Fr. Jacques Frémin (1628-1691) became a Jesuit in 1646 and worked among the Onondaga, Cayuga and Mohawk tribes, establishing the first

Catholic settlement on Isle LaMotte in Vermont. In 1668, he dedicated the first mission chapel among the Seneca, in the name of St. Michael the Archangel.[5]

Documented reports claim that Fr. Frémin was not of superior intellect and his social manners may have needed refinement; but his belief in Jesuit principles, his courage to persevere, and his common sense far outweighed any perceived deficiencies.[6]

Leaving only for journeys back to France to seek aid for his missions, he continued in service in Canada until his death in Quebec on July 2, 1691. It is believed he converted approximately 10,000 people in his lifetime.

The Iroquois-Huron War (1642-1698)
Who Were the Huron?

The Huron people lived in the northern Great Lakes region of North America. They founded a confederacy of their own called People of the Peninsula or Wendat which included four principal tribes: Bear, Rock, Barking Dogs, and White Thorns (also known as the Canoes).

In Huron culture, men could obtain wealth and position through war and trade. Traditionally, war was not waged among arguing tribes or against trespassing enemies solely to capture or retain territory. Most of the time, war broke out to repair the tainted honor of a warrior or to avenge an injury or an insult.

The people admired and respected their shrewd native traders almost as much as brave warriors. They valued this trading acumen because it displayed individual initiative and clever judgment. It took courage and diplomacy to pave new trade routes and/or to organize whole networks of alliances. If a native achieved wealth through trade, it was common practice not to possess or flaunt material goods, but instead be able to give them away. The Huron regarded divesting oneself of wealth as a method of improving social status.[7]

Europeans created one precious trade commodity—beaver fur. It had become fashionable for wealthy people on the European continent, especially in major cities like Paris and London, to have fur hats made for them. In sharp contrast to the mores of North American Indians, Europeans readily flaunted their wealth.

As the European demand for furs increased, both the Iroquois and the Huron began to expand north and westward in search of new animal populations and new Indian trading partners. This expansion also increased the number of violent conflicts between the two Nations. A formal trading alliance was proposed between the French and the Huron Confederacy as early as 1614. In this agreement, the Huron became allies of the French.

The Iroquois, who had been dealing with Dutch traders in New York, sent emissaries to Huron territory to offer peace and to also trade with the French. They intended to play two weighty European powers against each other to see who would come up with the most advantageous trade policies. The French became concerned the Iroquois would try to influence the Huron to start trading with the Dutch; and agreed to peace in 1622.[8]

In 1648, the Seneca and the Mohawk set out to destroy the Huron trading network. The Dutch armed the Seneca with firearms when they attacked the Huron town of Teanaostaiae. Warriors killed three-hundred and took 700 captive. The very next year, the collective Iroquois body attacked and destroyed the Huron, with a cache of 400 guns and unlimited ammunition supplied by the Dutch. This ended the Huron Confederacy. A new nation of displaced Huron refugees emerged, calling itself the Wyandot. They did not challenge the Iroquois—at least, not yet.

Blame it on Champlain?

The actual impetus for the Iroquois-Huron War (also called the Beaver Wars, the Iroquois Wars and the French and Iroquois Wars) might be ascribed to Samuel de Champlain (1567-1635) —French navigator, soldier, explorer, and cartographer. Early in the 17th century he led a band of Huron natives against their hereditary enemies, the Iroquois. (For more on the French and Indian Wars see Appendix E.)

The Huron were the original inhabitants of the St. Lawrence Valley in Quebec, Canada. "Huron" is the French name for the Wyandot people, who spoke their native Huron-Wendat, a language related to that of their many-times-removed Iroquois brethren; yet, the two entities remained distinctly opposed. Champlain helped keep this divide intact, by establishing trading companies that provided fur (and other desirable goods) to France. The lucrative fur trade had become extremely profitable and the notion of securing

Samuel de Champlain was a prominent figure in French exploration from 1603 to 1635 in the Americas.

a strong monopoly fueled the ambitious goals of the French government.

In the summer of 1609, Champlain attempted to solidify trade relations with the Huron and its allied tribes living along the St. Lawrence River. In return for their cooperation in securing precious beaver fur for him, the natives shrewdly demanded that he support them in their territorial war against the Iroquois, who had depleted their own land of beaver fur and began moving north into Wyandot territory to replenish their supply.

Champlain recruited 9 French soldiers and 300 natives to inspect an Iroquois settlement on the Riviere des Iroquois or what is now the Richelieu River. Having had no prior contact with the Iroquois, many men in his meager unit turned around and left, leaving Champlain with 2 Frenchmen and 60 natives. At the end of the month of July, what remained of Champlain's party encountered a group of Iroquois in the vicinity of Ticonderoga, New York. A written, documented entry in his diary read, "I had come with no other intention than to make war".

Two-hundred Iroquois advanced on Champlain's position just as one of his native guides identified 3 Iroquois chiefs. Champlain gingerly fired his gun—a muzzle-loaded firearm called an arquebus—killing two of the chiefs with a single shot to each. Following this, a shot fired from the gun of one of his men killed the third Iroquois chief. The Iroquois, who knew little of firearms, retreated, but this did not end the animosity. Rather, it reignited years of blistering hostilities.

It could be said that this single event, engineered by Champlain, would engender the most contentious and bloodthirsty enmity between the French and the Iroquois—the fiercest eastern warriors—for the remainder of the century.[9]

As for Champlain's historic contributions, he established the first French settlement, which is now Quebec and aided in the colonization of French North America, earning him the title, "The Father of New France". He did discover the elusive body of water explorers before him had missed, "Lake Champlain".

He was a noted cartographer and the first to produce an accurate map of the Canadian coastline and its surrounding areas.

The Seneca's Rise to Power in Western New York

As the Iroquois continued to move north, its ranks grew. The most numerous and adventurous member tribe, the Seneca, became the first to travel extensively. They explored parts of Delaware, Pennsylvania, Northern New Jersey, and back up again to their familiar stomping grounds, the Mid-Hudson Valley regions in Sullivan and Ulster counties in New York State. Using land and water routes through theses states, the Seneca became true traveling salesmen of their time, most prominently in the fur trade.

The American Revolutionary War

From the time Europeans first set foot on North American shores, native peoples traded, negotiated, and battled with them, trying to find and keep a mutually agreeable peace. In the process, various tribes employed tactics they hoped would work, even if it meant pitting the English and French against each other during the better part of the 1760s. The American Revolution emboldened natives even more, as the war presented them with new opportunities to do the same kind of "negotiating" with Americans and/or the British and their North American sympathizers. Some tribes wanted gifts and postwar promises from those with whom they would eventually support. Ultimately, most tribal nations allied with the British, who made sure to be in direct contact with them, offering blankets, knives, firearms, and alcohol—valuable items the natives had come to expect.

A Reluctant Seneca Chief Allies with Britain

Peace-minded Cornplanter, Seneca Warrior Chief, advocated for tribal neutrality in the American War, but sided perhaps reluctantly, with the British when the collective body of the Iroquois League (of which the Seneca comprised a major part) decided to do so. The 6 nations of the Iroquois League could comfortably produce 10,000 warriors for battle if they chose. American colonists knew this and hoped for tribal neutrality.

Retaliation: The Sullivan Campaign (1779)

In the summer of 1779, the American Congress supported George Washington in one of period's most ambitious and deadly strikes against the Iroquois warriors. Washington's army had been ordered to assault these tenacious British allies, forcing them out of New York. They situated their primary base of attack near present day Elmira, New York, in the heartland of the state. American general, John Sullivan, was appointed to lead 4,000 colonial soldiers in an invasion of Iroquois territory. This ambitious war initiative became known as the Sullivan Expedition. The company had been ordered to terrorize the Iroquois into a resounding defeat by completely destroying their homes and food supplies. Sullivan's men tore through more than 40 Cayuga and Seneca villages, burning them to the ground.[10]

For generations to come, natives recalling the attack referred to George Washington as "Town Destroyer." Sullivan later recorded in his war journal that "the immediate objects of this expedition are accomplished: total ruin of the Indian settlements and the destruction of their crops, which were designed for the support of those inhuman barbarians." [11]

At the close of the Revolution, intense bitterness continued between the warring parties. Despite social unrest and regret for his participation, Chief Cornplanter still worked toward reconciliation. He did not want to drag the Seneca into the fight in the beginning and steadily resisted the inevitable. But, once the decision was sealed, he bravely undertook his role as leader and warrior and committed himself to battle. When the war ended, Cornplanter resumed his mission to help build a lasting peace.

The Revolutionary War defied and successfully replaced the British Empire with the new American nation. The outcome, however, would be disastrous for American Indians. Britain had offered to negotiate geographic alliances with the natives; yet new Americans planned to expand their territory only by conquest or displacement. As the United States expanded west, so did New York.[12]

The Holland Land Purchase

"Enterprise, Industry, and Temperance cannot always ensure success
but the first of these will be felt by Society."
~ Inscription on gravestone of Oliver Phelps, 1809

Born in Windsor, Connecticut, Oliver Phelps (1749-1809) accumulated his fortune as a tavern keeper in Granville, Massachusetts. He was active in the American Revolution and commended by George Washington. When he entered into the Phelps-Gorham Land Purchase, many considered him to be the largest landowner in the country, with additional property holdings in Georgia, West Virginia, and Maine. He also founded the Hartford National bank and the held the position of its largest stockholder. He later moved to Canandaigua, New York, where he opened a grist mill. He was appointed as the first judge of Ontario County and served in the United States Congress between 1803-1805.[13]

Nathaniel Gorham (1738-1796) came from a modest, Massachusetts Bay colony family. He received a limited childhood education. At age 15 a New London, Connecticut merchant apprenticed him and he remained there for 6 years. When he returned to his home in Charlestown, Massachusetts, he opened his own mercantile businesses and married.

He eventually pursued a political career; first, as a public notary and subsequently became elected to the Colonial Legislature (1771-1775). He was a member of the Whig party during the American Revolution. He worked as a delegate to the Provincial Congress (1774-1775), a member of the Massachusetts Board of War (1778-1781), a delegate to the Constitutional Convention (1779-1780), and a representative to both Upper and Lower Houses, serving as speaker in 1781, 1782, and in 1785.

In 1788, Oliver Phelps and Nathaniel Gorham entered into the purchase of 6 million acres of Indian land in Western New York (from the Commonwealth of Massachusetts, as specified in the Treaty of 1786) for $1 million in Massachusetts "scrip". "Scrip" is a financial certificate that can be exchanged for a fractional share of stock.[14]

This piece of land stretched from the Pennsylvania border in the south, to the southern border of Lake Ontario in the north and from the Genesee River in western New York to the Seneca Lake in the east.

The transaction, which amounted to approximately $5,000 in New York value, or about one-half cent per acre, only cleared 2.6 million acres of Indian titled land, which Phelps and Gorham sold to white settlers. Overall, this devaluation caused a huge problem for these investors, as they based their purchase arrangement on the de-valued Massachusetts scrip. In time, the value of the scrip increased, but so did the value of the mortgage. A depressed land market put Phelps and Gorham in dire financial straits.

Phelps and Gorham died virtually penniless. Phelps died in debtor's prison and was buried at the Pioneer Cemetery in Canandaigua. His home was maintained and continues to stand on Main Street as the Oliver Phelps Country Inn.

Gorham suffered insolvency which led to his fall from high society and political esteem. He was buried at the Phipps Street Cemetery in Charlestown, Massachusetts.

Jesse Hawley: A Trickle of an Idea

A man named Jesse Hawley, originally from Connecticut, came to Canandaigua, New York, in 1796, working as a clerk in the office of Phelps and Gorham. He had also entered into a business partnership with Henry Corl of Geneva, New York, forwarding flour goods by boat along the unrefined and tediously long water systems in the area. The land was still undeveloped and shipping by water involved long, dangerous, and expensive hauls, especially in summer months when water levels fell to their lowest.

Hawley faced financial business challenges and was forced to default on the mortgage of his home. To make matters worse, Henry Corl declared bankruptcy and absconded with $10,000 of their partnership assets. In the winter of 1806, Hawley found himself incarcerated in debtor's prison in the Ontario County Jail and he began to compose a series of articles on how to better transport goods and people along New York's waterways, chiefly on what would become the Erie Canal.

He wrote 14 articles under the name "Hercules" and submitted them to the *Ontario Messenger* newspaper, now the *Daily Messenger*, which published them. Hawley's precise knowledge and explanation of the kind of engineering necessary to get such a canal up and running could be considered, perhaps, the basis for the most significant economic development in the history of New York State.[15]

The Holland Land Company

In 1792 and 1793 an unincorporated syndicate of Dutch land investors started the Holland Land Company. They purchased the western two-thirds (several million acres) of the Phelps and Gorham Purchase from Robert Morris, well-known as "the richest man in America". Three parties deliberated over the negotiations: Robert Morris represented by his son, Thomas, 1,000 Seneca Indians, and the United States government. This transaction is also known as the Holland Purchase.

But, before Morris could sell his land to the Holland Land Company, he had to dissolve the Indian's preemptive right to the land. He accomplished this at the Treaty of Big Tree in 1797.

Robert Morris (1734-1806)

Robert Morris was a founding father of the United States who financed the American Revolution and signed the Declaration of Independence.

Map of Western New York including the territories of the Holland Land purchase.

was an English-born American merchant who helped to finance the American Revolution against the British. He came from Pennsylvania and is considered a founding father of the United States of America, as he represented one of the 13 original British colonies who began the war effort, signed the Declaration of Independence, the Articles of Confederation, and the United States Constitution. He served in the Pennsylvania Assembly and as Chairman of the state's Committee of Safety. He also acted as a delegate to the Second Continental Congress.

From 1781 to 1784 he managed the financial economy of the United States, officiating next to General George Washington as Superintendent of Finance. His successful performance in this position earned him the nickname, "Financier of the Revolution". He also served voluntarily as Agent of the Marine, retaining powers similar to that of the Secretary of the Treasury.

This also placed him in control of the Continental Navy. He was one of Pennsylvania's original senators from 1789-1795.[16]

Putting One-Square-Foot in Front of the Other

Joseph Ellicott (1760 – 1826) was an American surveyor best known for laying out initial parcels of land purchased by The Holland Land Company in Batavia and Buffalo, New York. He also worked as a city planner, a land office agent, a lawyer, and a dedicated politician of the Quaker faith.

In 1797, The Holland Land Company hired Ellicott as Chief Surveyor. He had previously surveyed the company's land in northwestern Pennsylvania. After the Seneca's claim to the land had been removed, they assigned Ellicott the business of laying out the 3.3 million acres the company then owned, arranging specific boundaries for Seneca reservations, and sub-dividing all surrounding towns into 6-square-miles. This would be a daunting task.

Where natural land features permitted, Ellicott divided counties into townships measuring 8 miles by 8 miles. He then divided them into 64 lots, each 1 mile by 1 mile. He required surveyors to document these divisions in field log books, also describing the land, any waters, mill seats, valleys, mines, minerals or any other features which would be useful if/when the company decided to sell the land.

The largest obstacle Ellicott faced was to create a standard of measurement. Up until this time, the United States did not have such a standard. Starting from bare basics, Ellicott used a number of rulers to finally designate the 1-foot measurement as the standard we use today.

Next, he needed to come up with a portable transit instrument.

Joseph Ellicott- surveyor, city planner, land office agent and politician. He was instrumental in conducting surveys of Western New York for the Holland Land Purchase.

Ellicott's older brother, Andrew, also employed as a surveyor, used the only instrument of its kind in Florida, surveying the southern boundary between the United States and Spanish owned lands.

This curious device observed the paths of celestial bodies, and worked well in deep woods where a simple compass might not be as accurate. Another brother, Benjamin, built an entirely new transit instrument for use in the surveying of western New York.

Joseph Ellicott's tedious job started in March of 1798 and ended in October of 1800, costing The Holland Land Company over $70,000. The transit instrument he used is on display today at The Holland Land Office Museum in Batavia, New York.

A Prominent Advocate for the Erie Canal

Joseph Ellicott is also remembered as a firm supporter of the building of the Erie Canal and was among the Erie Canal Commissioners who supervised the canal construction in 1816. He arranged the contribution of more than 100,000 acres of land for the canal from The Holland Land Company.

Sometime between 1816 and 1817, Ellicott began to experience periods of depression, which may have contributed to an overall sense of hypochondria and uselessness. Some conjecture that this mental downslide resulted from financial strife connected to The Holland Land Company and the settlers they sold to, to his life as a single man, and/or to a rather empty, unfulfilling personal life.

In 1824 he was taken to New York's Bellevue Hospital, infamously noted for its treatment and housing of the mentally ill. Ellicott's condition deteriorated, psychologically and physically, and in 1826 he committed suicide by hanging. His remains were brought back to Batavia for burial.[17]

Ellicott's contributions are still very much in view and appreciated today in the layout of land in western New York; particularly in his 1804 plan for the city of Buffalo, with its original radial street design in Niagara Square.

The 100-Acre Tract That Could

Before Phelps and Gorham defaulted on their purchase agreement in 1790 and before the unsold portions of the purchase reverted back to the Commonwealth of Massachusetts, they gave the 100-acre land tract, known as the Mill Yard Tract, to Ebenezer "Indian" Allen, who did successfully build a grist mill and a sawmill there. (For more on Ebenezer "Indian Allan" see Appendix F) Allan built his sawmill first in the summer of 1789, then sawed timber to build his gristmill. He erected the frame in November of the same year. There, on the Upper Falls of what would become the prosperous city of Rochester, stood the beginnings of a thriving mill economy.

Dense wilderness surrounded the location of the 100-acre tract needed for its first mills. While construction continued, workers discovered the area to be infested with snakes and mosquitoes which spread Swamp Fever or what is commonly known as malaria.[18]

In March of 1792, with no settlers or land speculators interested in the surrounding land, Indian Allen sold the 100-acre tract to Benjamin Barton, Sr. of New Jersey for $1,250. Barton quickly resold the property to Samuel Ogden, an agent for Robert Morris. Ogden, in turn, sold the property in 1794 to Charles Williamson, agent for a small group of British investors called the Pulteney Association.

In 1803 the Association sold the 100-acre tract for $1,750 with a 5-year land contract, to Colonel Nathaniel Rochester and 2 lesser partners, Major Charles Carroll and Colonel William Fitzhugh, all of Hagerstown, Maryland.

Nathaniel Rochester, and associates, had just purchased the 100-acre tract that would become the city of Rochester, New York.[19]

Born in Westmoreland County, Virginia, Nathaniel Rochester (1752 - 1831) was an American Revolutionary War soldier and speculator His family moved to Granville County, North Carolina, when he was a child. As a young man, he became active in

Nathaniel Rochester- Revolutionary war soldier, most noted for founding the settlement which would become Rochester, New York.

civic organizations, served as a delegate to North Carolina's first Provincial Congress and later the North Carolina militia appointed him Major. In 1777 he was elected to the North Carolina General Assembly as county clerk. In 1780 he relocated to Hagerstown, Maryland, where he married and helped raise 12 children. In 1807, he founded the Hagerstown Bank and became its president. Two fellow bank directors, Colonel William Fitzhugh and Major Charles Carroll, discussed acquiring land in the new American frontier, specifically in the Genesee River area of New York State.

In 1811, Colonel Rochester began the process of establishing a town on the Upper Falls tract. Later that year, he began to offer plots for sale, naming the settlement "Rochesterville". During the War of 1812, settlers moved further inland in the area. In 1817, Rochester served on a committee to petition the state to build what would become the Erie Canal, with a proposed northern route across the Genesee River at Rochesterville. In 1821 Rochester held a pivotal position in the creation of Monroe County and became its first county clerk. He was subsequently elected as the county's first representative to the New York State Assembly. He remained active in town and county activities and became the first president of the Rochester Institute of Technology. During the last years of his life, he spent most of his time with family.[20]

Rochester's Upper Falls: One Sawmill, One Grist Mill

It wasn't until 1811 that Colonel Rochester and his partners completed payment for their purchase and received the deed to their mill-site property. The population of the area numbered a mere 15!

They had the tract surveyed and laid out into streets and land lots. A man named Henry Skinner purchased the very first lot—now the northwest corner of State and Main Streets. By 1817, other land owners such as the Brown Brothers (of Brown's Race and Brown's Square) linked their lands north to the 100-acre tract to form the Village of Rochesterville, which then boasted a population of 700.

From then on, the quickly blossoming seeds of what would become the city of Rochester spread and radiated from the original 100-acre tract. In 1821, Monroe County was formed from parts of Ontario and Genesee counties. Elisha Johnson purchased property to the east of the Genesee and across from the 100-acre tract, bringing Rochesterville's settled areas to 1,012 acres with a population of approximately 2,500. (See Appendix C)

The stage was now set for a series of events that would profoundly change not only the infrastructure of New York State but also the very character of America itself—the building of the Erie Canal.[21]

Chapter 5

A Little Short of Madness

The Erie Canal would change America. That was a certainty. The economic and social by-products of its construction could only be viewed as a much needed way to hurry trade and businesses along at an unprecedented clip, as well as provide a pleasurable and faster way for people to travel. It would, in more modern terms, bring the treasures and cultures of peoples of the world, together.

Visionaries: Were They All Wet?

Many men had visions; some ideas were sound in principle, some of them less conceivable. The brave perpetuity of an idea was the common denominator of the minds at the heart of the Erie Canal saga.

Who, exactly, rallied for its construction? Who were these people and what ideas did they propose? It may surprise you to learn the historical figures we traditionally assign to tasks of greatness—those who ultimately rise to the top of the completion of a historical marvel—followed a long list of equally deserving dream-makers.

It would take approximately 125 years for the Grand Canal to come to fruition. Its distinguished array of supporters—many of whom died before they could witness the reality—never failed to think of it as just that, a grand idea.

Sometimes, amid delayed ingenuity and intellectual consolation prizes, politics, opportunity, and timing propel an idea forward... even if it is just a little short of madness.

~

As early as 1699, Frenchman Sebastien Vauban (1633 –1707) suggested the benefit of linking lakes Erie and Ontario—presumably as a way of maintaining French dominance in North America—by a "cut across the Niagara Peninsula" via a series of canals and locks on the Mohawk River.[1]

Vauban is known as one of history's first modern civil engineers. He built and secured fortresses in war time with expert talent. As French trade developed, so did France's scientific strides in the fields of coastal engineering and marine hydraulic science. Vauban's conversion of Dunkirk

Cadwallader Colden- physician, farmer, surveyor, botanist and a Lieutenant Governor for the Providence of New York. He was considered to be the father of the canal system.

into an impregnable coastal fortress became his most eminent public works project. He also made improvements in 1692 to the Midi Canal (also called the Languedoc Canal, French Canal du Midi or Canal du Languedoc) which served local French trade.[2]

In 1724 many considered, Scottish born American, Cadwallader Colden (1688-1776), to be among the most learned men in colonial America. He has also been called the "Father of the Canal System".

Colden worked a medical doctor and he identified improper sanitation as the primary cause of an outbreak of Yellow Fever (The Great Disease) in 1741. He often walked the streets of New York City, treating victims of the widespread, debilitating illness. He concluded that its causes stemmed from urban woes, specifically, poor drainage of dirty water, human handling of impure soil, and the breathing in of polluted air.

At the time, Manhattan Island was not only described as being surrounded by water, but also as being encircled by sewage. Colden recommended better ventilation systems, improvement of the water quality, and the construction of a public drainage system.

Appointed Surveyor General of New York in 1720, this set the stage for his future regard as a genuine colonial scholar and principal political leader. In 1721, he became a member of the New York Governor's Council.

In 1724, he presented to colonial governor, William Burnett, the advantages of utilizing the topography and natural streams and rivers of New York, as the perfect sites for a canal between the Hudson River and the Great Lakes. This would speed up trade (of fur and agricultural goods) among native populations and western settlers.[3]

Colden's book, *The History of the Five Indian Nations*, published in 1727 and thought to be the first history book published in America, became a valuable resource on the Iroquois tribes and their democratic form of government. The Mohawk Nation "adopted" him and he peacefully traveled throughout Iroquois territory, having earned the admiration of these Native Americans.

In 1751, he critiqued Newton's theory of gravity in *The Principle of Action in Matter*, becoming a world-renowned botanist of the new Linnaean system of classifying flora and fauna. It is reported that he also provided technical advice and counsel to Benjamin Franklin concerning his own scientific theories.

In 1761, he rose to Lieutenant Governor of New York, which placed him in an advantageous position to order sanitization of the city's water supply, thus improving public health.[4]

An "Over the Top" Idea?

"Had I been brought up as a hatter, people would have come into the world without heads," opined Christopher Colles (1789-1816), American engineer and inventor, in attributing the failure of the majority of his projects to bad luck.

Of all the personalities involved in the Erie Canal story, Colles is one of the most colorful. Many of his contemporaries thought of him as "ingenious", as "one of those gifted men whose misfortune consists in being ahead of their times", and as "being so ambitious in so young and unestablished a country".

Colles worked on a water distribution system in New York City prior to the beginning of the Revolutionary War. The system used a steam-engine-driven pump to extract water, a reservoir to store it, and adequate piping to distribute it throughout the city. But, the project came to a halt when the British invaded the city in 1776.

In 1775, he presented a plan to improve the waterways of the Mohawk Valley, to the New York State

Christopher Colles, inventor and engineer, was widely credited with being the first to conceive of a waterway to the west.

legislature. In a pamphlet entitled Proposal for the Speedy Settlement of the Waste and Unappropriated Lands on the Western Frontiers of the State of New York, Colles proposed the construction of a series of canals and locks along the Mohawk River that would connect the Hudson River and Lake Ontario. The canals would link the Atlantic Ocean with the interior of North America and guarantee "the speedy settlement" of the frontier. The New York State legislature, however, would only allow the proposal if the plan could be privately funded. This did not materialize and he abandoned the project.

Colles' most ambitious idea again involved building a canal... with a twist. He proposed the Timber Canal—a canal built entirely of timber and elevated to run above ground. Colles detailed the imaginative project in a pamphlet called *Proposal for a Design for the Promotion of the Interests of the United States* (1808). In this he explained how an over-ground canal would bypass "enormous roots of trees (which) make digging expensive" and would make good use of "immense forests (and) timber in abundance now constantly burning and rotting away."

The plan began with a single route across New Jersey; the route would extend from the Navesink River (an 8-mile-long estuary in Monmouth County,

New Jersey), then proceed westward to the Delaware River. Of all his projects, the Timber Canal was the most revolutionary and, therefore, the least likely to be achieved. The project never moved forward. Yet, Christopher Colles would be credited as being the first to conceive of a waterway to the West, a feat that would ultimately be achieved by the Erie Canal.[5]

Elkanah Watson (1758–1842), tenacious businessman, banker, land speculator, and agriculturist, also staunchly supported the construction of a commercial canal in western New York State.

In 1791, Jeremiah Van Rensselaer (an opposer of the Federal Constitution and a supporter of American liberties) joined him along with Philip Van Cordtlandt (wealthy surveyor and landowner) and Stephen Bayard (a former mayor of New York City) on an expedition through western New York. They wanted explore the possibility of building a canal to connect the Hudson River with Lake Erie. Watson then submitted a proposal to the New York State Legislature to use the states waterways to connect the Hudson River to New York City and westward to the Great Lakes.

Watson maintained that he should be justly credited as the sole creator of the concept that would result in the building of the Erie Canal. This position would bring him into a longstanding, bitter conflict with the future New York State governor, DeWitt Clinton, who also claimed his own future initiative as being first.[6]

~

In 1792, the Holland Land Company acquired huge land tracts in the Genesee River region of New York State and invested in the newly chartered Western Inland Lock and Navigation Company, owned by company president Philip Schuyler (1733–1804).

Schuyler was deeply involved in the commercial development of New York, having overseen the construction of saw mills, gristmills, and New York's first flax mill. In addition, he exported timber and other products via the Hudson River and would quite naturally take a leading role in the development of better commercial transportation in the state.

Schuyler was a distinguished member of New York State's landed aristocracy and the father-in-law of Alexander Hamilton. He also served as a general in the American Revolution and one of the first United States senators from New York. Elkanah Watson needed this politically prominent figure to push his proposal forward so he convinced Schuyler to take his concept of a western canal to the New York State Legislature. Schuyler strongly defended its necessity and the two men became business partners.

As president and major decision-maker in the creation and incorporation of the Western Inland Lock and Navigation Company, Schuyler first concentrated on the improvement of the water route from Schenectady to Oneida Lake. To do this they would have to battle the twisted, narrow channel called Wood Creek. This troublesome body of water connected the west end of the canal area at Rome, New York, and the east end of Oneida Lake. Travelers reported that the stream at Wood Creek became so narrow they could actually jump across it!

Philip Schuyler- father-in-law of Alexander Hamilton. He was president of the Western Inland Lock and Navigation Company.

Nevertheless, it remained the lynch pin of the water route to the Great Lakes.

Schuyler's company constructed a series of dams, locks, and short canal segments along the Mohawk River and across the tricky Wood Creek divide at Rome. This allowed shallow, flat-bottomed boats to carry cargo from Schenectady to the Oneida Lake, and on to the Finger Lakes and Lake Ontario. These accomplishments would be expanded as the basis of the Erie Canal system.[7]

Robert Fulton: Before the Steamboat

American engineer and inventor, Robert Fulton (1765-1815), always had a penchant for experimenting with mechanical inventions. He focused, however, in the construction and engineering of boats and how to make them move.

Fulton, of course, is credited with developing the first commercially successful steamboat, the Clermont, in 1807.

In 1793, as a mediocre student of fine art in England, Fulton felt drawn to the "Canal Mania" stirring in New York. He turned his talents to developing an inclined plane system—instead of locks—for hauling canal boats over difficult terrain. He received an English patent for the inclined plane system in 1794. His benefactor, Robert Owen, recommended him to a canal company in Manchester, England, who hired Fulton as a sub-contractor. He soon abandoned the position because he believed it did not provide an ongoing opportunity to invent and be funded, at the same time.

Robert Fulton, engineer and inventor, is widely credited with developing a commercially successful steam boat. He was also instrumental in raising awareness of the feasibility of canal construction and locks.

These developments culminated in Fulton's publication, in 1796, of a *Treatise on the Improvement of Canal Navigation*, written while he still lived in England. He sent a copy of the report to President George Washington in the United States. With this he included a letter detailing how the "creative canal system" he originally designed to connect Lancaster to Philadelphia, Pennsylvania, and to Lake Erie in the United States, could and should be expanded many times over to involve all the states from the east coast to the west coast. At the time, the contents of Fulton's letter provided the first historical record to suggest a canal connecting Philadelphia and Lake Erie.

His letter also included innovative business ideas. These placed Fulton's economic predictions and positive social outcomes—resulting from the use of canals for trade and travel—far into a successful and profitable American future, never before described.[8]

In Fulton's correspondence with Washington, he not only enumerated exactly how the mechanical features of the canals would operate, but also asked for the president's endorsement (and early marketing) of such a project. He wrote, "That your Excellencies' Sanction will awaken Public Attention to the Subject".

While Fulton's ideas appeared radical then, they made sense. Highlights of his letter to President George Washington included the creation of member or "subscriber" companies in each state. The managers and workers would apply a percentage of their salaries or profits to a fund dedicated to produce ongoing work in the construction of chains of canals throughout the country. This may have been the earliest description of communal profit sharing or shareholding.

He proposed a traveling toll, initially intended for Pennsylvania, which he estimated as yielding approximately $4 million dollars per year. Also, applying a percentage of profits from a public utility (a canal) to consistently extend canal construction was another idea far beyond its time. Many felt the prediction that in 60 to 70 years from this proposal, Pennsylvania, for example, would have 9,360 miles of canal at its disposal, "bringing water carriage within easy reach of every house within 10 miles of a canal" . . . instead of "turnpike systems or river navigations that lead to nowhere" as incomprehensible.

Another result of canal construction and increased water travel, Fulton advised, "Would bind the whole (society) in the bonds of social intercourse." He believed that this improved method of transportation would prove to be crucial to the country's progress and would be the greatest "leveler" of domestic and international economic and social dissension.

Fulton's advice to Washington was "internal improvement" of the country which depended on promoting agriculture, manufacturing, and the use of manual labor.[9]

By Fits and Starts: A Vision of the Future

Schuyler's Western Inland Lock Navigation Company began work on the canal. By 1796, it had already built 5 locks at Little Falls (east of Utica in Herkimer County, New York), spanning 2¾ miles; and a 1¼ mile canal at German Flatts, southeast of Utica. Another 2-mile-long canal had been constructed from the Mohawk River to Wood Creek.

The canal had original dimensions of 26-feet-wide at the bottom, 35-feet-wide on the surface, and a depth of 3-feet. Sixteen-ton boats already sailed between Schenectady and Seneca Lake. The Western Inland Lock Navigation Company had been given a $15,000 loan from the state to begin its work. The following year, the company secured an additional $250,000 loan to continue its work.

Before the project neared completion, its cost had already totaled $480,000 opposed to its original erroneous estimate of approximately $200,000. Within 6 years, the locks built of wood (a more expensive material) had to be rebuilt and reinforced with bricks and mortar.[10]

In 1798, the state incorporated and gave authority to the Niagara Canal Company to construct a canal from Lake Erie to Lake Ontario; 6-miles-long with 50 locks and a surface area of 70-feet by 16-feet by 4-feet deep.

Hello, Hawley

Jesse Hawley. While in debtor's prison and writing under the name of Hercules, he published essays on the idea of a canal from the Hudson River to Lake Erie.

Remember unfortunate Jesse Hawley as he sat in debtor's prison for defaulting on the mortgage of his home, after his business partner disappeared with their profits?

During his incarceration (1807 to 1808) in the Ontario County Jail, Hawley composed a series of 14 articles which detailed, with astounding precision and accuracy, how to use New York's waterways to build the kind of canal that would galvanize the economic prowess of America. He sent his articles, which he called "numbers", to the *Ontario Messenger* newspaper (today, the *Daily Messenger*). The *Messenger* published the articles under his pen name, "Hercules".

The first essay of his Herculean initiative introduced the proposition of "A Canal from the Foot of Lake Erie into the Mohawk", predicated on an inclined plane plan. In formulating the physical feasibility of such a project, he compared New York's potential use of natural resources to those of England, France, and in particular, China.

He estimated the canal would take approximately 1 year to build. It would be paid for by citizens and the federal government using "surplus revenue of the United States". A minimal state tax would be imposed for the use and improvement of roads and other lesser canals and highways of transportation. The design of the canal measured approximately 100-feet by 10-feet. Hawley advised that the location of the canal should be as close as possible to the "fall" of the Niagara River to keep a steady "fountain" supply of natural water available at all times.

The daunting, though navigable route, when completed, would run from the canal's primary location at the rivers' junction to Albany, from Albany to Buffalo, and from Buffalo to Chicago and back. Hawley concluded that freight charges and additional duty (tax) from Canadian trade alone, would defray the annual cost of repairs to the canal and he predicted that within 27 years, the principal and interest fees would be paid in full. He also included Boston harbor on the east coast in the growing canal network, which would connect waterways north and south of New York. He believed that the New Jersey coast should also be included in this stretch, by opening a passage between Delaware and the Hudson River.

Hawley was also keenly aware of "the resources of capital present in our forests", specifically "pot-ash"—the result of soaking plant ashes in water to extract potassium—and the benefits of manufacturing and trading New York-produced salt. The increased sale and transport of these two valuable materials would create the necessity for a viable commercial waterway.

Basing his figures on the construction of the Languedoc Canal in France and on the Canal of Clyde in England, he estimated the cost of the New York canal to be approximately $6 million—or $30 thousand per mile—or $93.75 per rod.[11]

(The actual cost of the Erie Canal was in the neighborhood of $7,600,000.)

Jesse Hawley's Letter to Erastus Granger

All rivers, lakes and streams—accompanied by a myriad of historical personalities—seemed destined to meet again in the rush of Canal Mania.

In 1804, Erastus Granger moved from Connecticut to Buffalo as one of its original settlers. His cousin, Gideon Granger, worked as the Postmaster-General of the United States under President Thomas Jefferson. Erastus was appointed Superintendent of Indian Affairs and shortly afterwards, as the first postmaster of Buffalo. He also assumed the duties of Collector of Port, in charge of collecting import duties on goods entering the United States by ship at the port of Buffalo.

Records indicate two interesting facts about his work. First, as postmaster, it appeared he had been entrusted with the general politics in Buffalo and subsequently led the Republican Party on the Niagara frontier. Second, he was commissioned to test the water levels of Lake Erie; this temporary assignment only applied to the possibility that a canal would be built. This last piece of information spurred a reaction from Jesse Hawley—who was a fellow merchant and friend of Erastus Granger.

Just prior to arriving at the Ontario County Jail to fulfill his term in debtor's prison, Hawley wrote a letter to Granger. In it, he mentioned the establishment of an overland canal; but claimed to "have no individual interest in the subject", yet, he felt compelled to share "superficial" information on the topic. Curiously, he also questioned why water levels had only been taken from Lake Erie and not from other bodies of water, such as Lake Ontario. Did Hawley plan to compose his series of essays before he entered prison? Or, did he want to test the political waters by writing to Granger? And, Hawley deeply researched geographical and financial calculations, often down to the inch and the penny; making it odd he called the information "superficial".

His comments to Granger included examples of the building and maintenance of successful canals in France and Denmark, and how much all of it cost. In fact, the tone of his letter would lead a reader to believe, in his opinion, that money should not be an object and the cost to build a canal might be less than the examples he cited, as evidenced by his exacting figures.

Hawley did have a lot of time on his hands to gather an abundance of facts and figures; 14 essays later, it would have been natural for him to look for support from government sectors—and friends in government. Ultimately, his extensive written proposal(s) would be deemed the first of their kind to address the creation of a canal with such overriding sophistication and accuracy.[12]

Albert Gallatin:
By Land and by Sea

"The Age of Canals" also witnessed the exploration of ways to maximize land travel in the United States. Albert Gallatin (1761-1849), Secretary of the Treasury under Thomas Jefferson's, and author of the landmark article of 1808 entitled *Report on Roads, Canals, Harbors, and Rivers*, prominently advocated for better internal road systems

With political attention focusing on the construction of water transportation, the treacherous conditions of

Albert Gallatin. He wrote the 1808 landmark, *Reports on Roads, Canals, Harbors, and Rivers*. The report was astounding in its scope and led to array of infrastructure projects that took 100 years to complete.

America's inland roadways took a back seat, as did their potential to advance commerce and travel.

Also known as "The Father of the National Road", Gallatin understood that in order for the United States to take its place as a major nation, it needed to develop superior inter-state turnpike systems, as well as maximize the use of its waterways with canals. His startling and far-reaching report urged Congress to expend $16 million on extensive road work and numerous canals throughout the United States and proposed the novel idea of borrowing ahead of tax revenues.

His 100-page report suggested the creation of "infrastructure projects", a concept far ahead of its time. Its recommendations would come under the modern category of a national broadband plan, which defines a road-map of initiatives to stimulate economic growth, thus allowing for the full realization of a country's capabilities.[13]

Jefferson had been elected president primarily for his platform of limited federal government and he rejected Gallatin's plan until the War of 1812 subsided. However, Gallatin's efforts to retire the federal debt and begin any of the projects he advised also subsided.

"You will have learned that an act for internal improvement, after passing both Houses, was negatived by the President", wrote Jefferson to Gallatin.

"The act was founded, avowedly, on the principle that the phrase in the Constitution which authorizes Congress 'to lay taxes to pay the debts and provide for the general welfare,' was an extension of the powers specifically enumerated to whatever would promote the general welfare...

I think the passage and rejection of this bill a fortunate incident... [it] will settle forever the meaning of this phrase, which, by a mere grammatical quibble, has countenanced the General Government in a claim of universal powers."[14]

Gallatin's Plan

The major points of Gallatin's plan included a turnpike from Maine to Georgia, a series of canals on the Atlantic coast from New York City to South Carolina, a series of networking canals to Ohio and a canal crossing New York State; it also encompassed river navigation improvements to the Potomac, the Susquehanna, the James, and the Santee. He suggested spending $2 million each year for 10 years while selling stock in the country's turnpikes and canals to fund their upkeep and future improvements.

The Erie Canal would be among such projects financed by state and private monies.

The Realities of Gallatin's Plan

The realities of Gallatin's plan included intra-coastal waterway travel, an early version of our interstate highway system, and one major road project, the National Road. Also called the Cumberland Road (1811), the road began in Cumberland, Maryland and moved eastward toward Washington, DC and westward toward Indiana. Today, it is US route 40 and it extends to the west coast.[15]

Keeping the Dream Afloat

Jonas Platt (1769-1834) came to the rescue of his friend, Thomas Eddy (1758-1827), treasurer of The Western Inland Lock Navigation Company in 1797, when his company suffered financial setbacks in its attempt to forge a navigable route from the Mohawk River to Lake Ontario in possible preparation for a canal.

Platt served as a New York State senator and leader of the Federalist Party. He believed a canal was surely warranted. Together, the two men agreed on the contents of a proposal to the New York State Legislature calling for the creation of a bipartisan commission to investigate two possible canal routes extending to either Lake Ontario or Lake Erie. On March 13, 1810, Platt presented the proposal which received overwhelming support.[16]

Jefferson and the Mad Men

William Kirkpatrick (1769-1832), a member of the United States House of Representatives, and New York State Assemblyman, Joshua Forman (1777-1849), supported the canal. Forman was, in fact, said to have been elected to the New York State Legislature on the "Canal Ticket".

Forman followed Hawley's published essays and came to support the practicality of his proposals and the need for a commissioned group to survey the water routes in question. Forman and Kirkpatrick even traveled to Washington, DC, "making a Federal case" to President Thomas Jefferson for the building of a canal.

At their meeting, Forman enumerated the advantages of constructing a canal, including the enhanced value of existing settlers' land and an attraction for new settlements. He proposed it would open commercial channels to the west; provide a military station in time of war, and the overall bond the American people and their states.[17]

Jefferson agreed that the project had merit, but "might be executed a century hence." He continued:

> "Why sir, here is a canal of a few miles (in Washington), projected by General Washington, which, if completed, would render this a fine commercial city—which has languished for many years because the small sum of $200,000 necessary to complete it, cannot be

obtained from the general government, the state government, or from individuals—and you talk of making a canal of 350 miles through the wilderness—it is little short of madness to think of it at this day."[18]

~

The accuracy of his comment would later be referenced by his contemporaries who reported that although Jefferson did not recall his exact words, he did confirm that he had "no doubt" said them or something similar.

In November of 1822, amid construction of the Erie Canal, DeWitt Clinton wrote to Jefferson, relating a version of the story told by Forman after their meeting in 1809. Jefferson replied to Clinton with the following: "Altho' I do not recollect the conversation with Judge Forman referred to . . . I have no doubt it is correct; for that I know was my early opinion, and many, I dare say still think with me that N. York has anticipated by a full century the ordinary progress of improvement."

The Erie Canal Commission (1810)

The formation of the Erie Canal Commission in 1810 became a concrete, pivotal chapter in the canal's history. This enormous move forward would yield far-reaching, life-changing results. Not only would this effort hold its appointed commissioners to high standards of researching all aspects of building the canal, it also gave the project political credibility and served as affirmation to its "mad men" and supporters.

When Thomas Eddy expanded Joshua Forman's original idea of building a canal linking key rivers rather than attempting to find a way to navigate them, he found an eager and politically connected participant in Jonas Platt. Both men also knew that appointees to such a commission had to command a certain degree of social and political stature.[19]

The bipartisan Erie Canal Commission was formed on March 15, 1810, just two days after the legislature approved Platt's proposal, with an appropriation of $3,000 at the outset. Governor Morris, Stephen Van Rensselaer, William North and Thomas Eddy made up the appointed Federalist members. Democratic-Republican appointees were DeWitt Clinton, Simeon DeWitt, and Peter Buell Porter.

They needed to accomplish what had been talked about for so long, to explore the feasibility of a route of inland navigation from the Hudson River to Lake Ontario and Lake Erie and submit their findings.

They first faced the challenge of traveling west to survey the land and probable route for the canal. One of the original appointees, Governor Morris filled the position of the new president of the commission. His title was somewhat ceremonial, as most members looked to DeWitt Clinton for practical guidance. Morris and Van Rensselaer made the trip by carriage; the others traveled up the Mohawk River as far as possible, where two surveyors, James Geddes and Benjamin Wright, joined them. The group then traveled the final 100 miles from Lake Seneca to Lake Erie by carriage. Clinton kept a prolific journal of the entire trip, painstakingly recording each development along the way.[20]

The Report of the Erie Canal Commission (1811)

One year later, the Erie Canal Commission reported their recommendation for an inland route that would run directly to Lake Erie. They decided that if the canal's route headed any other way, the St. Lawrence River would still be the primary route of transportation, and would not connect the east and west. Additionally, Morris' proposal for a natural waterway, created from Lake Erie's overflow—versus the artificial waterway of a canal—was rejected.

Most important, the new commission would demand public funding, in the form of land grants and related loans, in addition to securing financing from Congress and other states. Finally, the control and ownership of the canal would rest solely with the State of New York.

The state legislature issued a canal law, reappointing the canal board and appropriating $15,000. They also authorized the commission to negotiate the purchase of the failed Western Inland Lock Navigation Company and to oversee the construction of the canal.[21]

Benjamin Wright (1770 –1842): Constructing the Erie Canal

Benjamin Wright assumed the position of chief civil engineer in the construction of the Erie Canal. While working with renowned English canal designer, William Weston (a consultant to the Erie Canal Commission), Wright laid out canals and locks on the Mohawk River. The Western Inland Lock Navigation Company also commissioned him to survey the Mohawk River between Schenectady and Rome, and on to the Hudson River; however, the project lacked sufficient financial resources. In 1811, he again surveyed the same route under the auspices of the Erie Canal Commission. By 1816, funding had been accomplished and construction began in 1817.

He managed thousands of unskilled laborers, as they wielded wheelbarrows, hand tools, horses, and mules in the painstaking tasks of clearing land. The Chief Engineer, named in Wrights honor, became first boat to navigate the canal system was named the Chief Engineer in Wright's honor.

Benjamin Wright was the chief engineer of the Erie Canal. In 1969, the American Society of Civil Engineers declared him the "Father of American Civil Engineering."

Later, he worked as a consultant to other canal projects and began surveying for railroads projects. He was elected to the New York State Legislature and eventually appointed as a New York county judge. In 1969, the American Society of Civil Engineers (ASCE) declared him the "Father of American Civil Engineering".[22]

That Charm Called Politics

"The overflowing blessings from this fountain of public good and national abundance will be as extensive as our own country and as durable as time".

~ DeWitt Clinton

History buffs would most likely agree that when stupendous strides or disastrous decisions are made by a particular political administration—be it the activity of a sitting mayor, or governor, or even President of a nation—the individual in charge is credited with the achievement or blamed for the failure.

DeWitt Clinton (1769-1828), New York's 6th governor, will forever be remembered as the man who turned the much talked about, much ridiculed and derided, but never forgotten—Erie Canal—into a shining, historic reality.

~

Clinton was of Dutch ancestry and born in New York into a family actively involved in politics. Clinton's education, career appointments, and the experience of family members prepared him for a life in government.

Dewitt Clinton served as a United States Senator and sixth Governor of New York. Clinton believed infrastructure improvements could transform American life.

He received his education at King's College, which later became Columbia University, after transferring from Princeton University. He graduated in 1790 with a law degree, the first student to do so under the university's new name. He was admitted to the bar in the same year. Immediately following, he became private secretary to his uncle, George Clinton (1797-1798), the then acting governor of New York. The young Clinton joined the Democratic-Republican Party. His brother, George Clinton, Jr. and his half-brother, James G. Clinton, both served in Congress.[23]

He served in the New York State Assembly, the New York Senate (1798 -1802), and in the United States Senate (1802-1803). He worked as a delegate to the New York State Constitutional Convention in 1801 and a member of the Council of Appointments from 1801 to 1802 and from 1806 to 1807.

Clinton also governed as mayor of New York City for 10 terms—from 1803 to 1807, 1808 to 1810, and 1811 to 1815. He focused on public education, city planning, manufacturing, public sanitation, and aid for the impoverished. As mayor, he organized the Historical Society of New York (1804) and served as its president. His interest in the arts and the natural sciences provided him the impetus to organize the American Academy of Fine Arts (1808) and act as its president, from 1813 and 1817. He was a Regent (part of the governing body) of the University of New York from 1808 to 1825. He became an elected member of the American Antiquarian Society in 1814 and served as its vice-president from 1821 to 1828. He founded the New York Literary and Philosophical Society and was vice-president of the American Bible Society. He also authored several works, including *An Introductory Discourse Before the N.Y. Historical Society* (1814), *Memoirs on the Antiquities of Western New York, Letters on the Natural History and Internal Resources of New York* (1818), and *Speeches to the Legislature* (1823).

From 1810 to1824, Clinton served as an integral member of the Erie Canal Commission.[24]

After the death in 1811 of Lieutenant Governor of New York, John Broome, Clinton assumed the office until 1813. In 1812, he ran for President of the United States, but James Madison beat him by a narrow margin.

Then, in 1817, after the resignation of Daniel D. Tompkins as governor of New York, a special election named DeWitt Clinton as governor. He took office on July 1, 1817. Re-elected in 1822, he served until December 31st of that year. During his last term as governor, Clinton continued to promote on the state level the causes he initiated as mayor of New York, with the addition of instituting legal reform in the state. Throughout his career(s), Clinton vehemently opposed slavery in the United States and strongly supported its abolition.

Clinton married Maria Franklin, the daughter of a prominent New York Quaker merchant, in February of 1796 and became the father of 10 children. She passed away in 1818. In the spring of the following year, he married Catherine Jones, the daughter of a New York physician. Clinton's son, George William Clinton (1807-1885), served as mayor of Buffalo, New York, from 1842 to 1843.

DeWitt Clinton died in 1828 of heart failure. While seen as an astute, respected politician, he failed at managing his personal finances, leaving his family in poor monetary straits. It took 16 years for them to collect enough money to purchase a suitable grave-site. He was finally interred at the Green-

Wood Cemetery in Brooklyn, New York; it is one of the first rural cemeteries in America and now a National Historic Landmark. Happily, Governor DeWitt Clinton lived to see and celebrate the completion of his cherished canal.

Political and Personal Perseverance

Commonly referred to as "The Father of the Erie Canal", Clinton held steady in his belief that the canal would provide crucial advancement of his state, and he backed this with his political standing. Fighting tirelessly for New York to join the ranks of those states that were home to important ports, such as Boston in Massachusetts and Philadelphia in Pennsylvania, he never faltered in his efforts.

Because the canal would connect the Great Lakes with the Atlantic Ocean, those states farther west would benefit as well as New York; thus, the federal government was asked to pay for the cost of construction. Congress refused to have anything to do with the project.

To keep the issue alive, Clinton began a Canal Fund, enlisting the support of former rival, Martin Van Buren, in the state senate, along with other legislators and farmers. Drawing on American nationalism and republicanism in his appeal, Clinton presented a popular memorandum known as the "New York Memorial"—bearing over 1,000 signatures of New York State residents—to the legislature calling for the building of the canal. Land surveys continued, the discussion of finances began again, the training of engineers in England and Holland also began, but in 1816, plans to go forward stalled when President James Madison vetoed the Bonus Bill—the key to national funding. Luckily, in an unexpected way, the veto of the Bonus Bill fired up New Yorkers' sense of resolution and commitment to the canal and by April of 1817, the canal bill passed, guaranteeing finances for the completion of the project. On July 4, 1817, crews broke ground at Utica, New York, as construction began both to the east and to the west.[25]

~

It would take seven years of back breaking labor to manually remove shovels and buckets of earth in a 363-mile span across New York State's wilderness—the longest distance ever attempted in the United States. A continued backdrop of bickering, partisan infighting, and reiteration of the outrageous estimated price tag of nearly $7.5 million shadowed the project.

Naysayers doubted the efficacy of the Erie Canal. They claimed that the labor involved, topped by the overwhelming cost, far outweighed the importance of the 4-foot deep, 40-foot wide "ditch" in question.

A Vision Brought Into Focus

The Erie Canal's unparalleled success seemed to appear almost overnight. In its first year of operation, the canal turned a handsome profit, providing the state of New York with impressive revenues and a positive impact on the daily activities winding across the state. Even with the rise of railroad construction and travel, the Erie Canal thrived, carving out new settlement and economic patterns.

It made New York City the financial and commercial capital of the world. Its advantageous location also offered a critical supply network in the North during the Civil War. The Erie Canal was considered the engineering marvel of the 19th century and a brilliant mechanism for American nationalism.

The Effects of the Finished Product

The Erie Canal dramatically and quickly facilitated settlements in and around western New York and further into the western states, offering access to rich land and natural resources west of the Appalachian Mountains.

Early in the 19th century, long days or even weeks of laborious travel physically removed people living in the capital city of Albany in the western part of New York State. Granted, there was a water route between Cayuga and Seneca Lakes to Schenectady, and primitive roads laced across the state, but traders limited transactions largely to coastal areas. From a businessman's point of view, these conditions ate into one's pocket and into one's economic future.

Even with this water route available, it could often take a full three weeks, or more—and greater than the going rate of $10—to haul a barrel of flour from Albany to Buffalo.

From the outset, the canal welcomed enormous strides in freight and passenger travel. These accomplished goals almost immediately benefited merchants, especially when the freight cost between Buffalo and Albany fell from $100 per ton by road to $10 per ton by water. At one point, the charge for carrying a barrel of flour across the state was reduced to 30 cents; and a bushel of wheat could travel from Buffalo to New York City for 4 to 5 cents! The tolls along the canal route also began to enable New York State to recoup the money spent on the massive project.

In the first 15 years of the canal's existence, New York became the busiest port in America, handling tonnages greater than Boston, Baltimore, and New Orleans, combined. The similar impact on New York's other cities—with the exception of Binghamton and Elmira—showed that every major city in New York was situated along the trade route originally established by the Erie Canal, from New York City, to Albany, through Schenectady, Utica, Syracuse, Rochester and Buffalo. The success of the Erie Canal encouraged New York's "Canal Boom" of the mid-1800s, as the lateral canals on Lakes Champlain, Oswego, and the Cayuga-Seneca also flourished.

By1829, just four years after the completion of the canal, 3,640 bushels of wheat had been transported from Buffalo. By 1837, in less than an additional ten-year period, this transported figure increased to 500,000 bushels; 4 years later, the figure soared to 1 million bushels. In less than a decade, the canal tolls had paid for the entire cost of the construction of the Erie Canal.[26]

The Details and Detriments

When digging for the first part of the canal began in Rome, New York, on July 4, 1817, curiously, workers dug the middle section of the canal first. Reports suggested that friends of the canal at either end would insist their section be finished next, which explained the reason for this odd choice. From a practical viewpoint, it would also deter the efforts of canal opposers to interfere with the work in progress.

At the time of its completion, the Erie Canal had become the second longest artificial waterway in the world, only a canal in China proved to be longer. Its dimensions were 363-miles long, forty-feet wide at the surface, 28-feet wide at the bottom, with a depth of 4-feet of water. It had 83 locks with a total lockage of 655 feet. The water cascaded to the east in all of the locks, except for 27-miles near Syracuse, where it fell to 46-feet to the west, leaving the actual descent from Buffalo to Albany 563-feet. The largest boats to pass

A Little Short of Madness

"Lockport, Erie Canal", a painting by W.H. Bartlett, 1839. The view is looking east from the eastbound lock.

through the canal averaged at 76-tons burden.

Among the horrendous impediments to the mammoth physical tasks required to prepare for the canal stood nature's ancient rock formations, thickly rooted trees, leathery grass, and swamp-like areas. The first obstacle involved crossing the awkwardly situated Irondequoit Creek and the Genesee River near Rochester. Rectifying the situation meant building an immense 1,320-foot structure called the "Great Embankment", a necessary achievement which would carry the canal to a height of 76-feet above the creek and through a 245-foot culvert, below. When finished a stone aqueduct 802-feet long, 17-feet wide with 11 arches crossed the river.

One of the most problematical developments during construction would be overcoming the 70-foot shift in elevation called the Niagara Escarpment. This seemingly impenetrable formation of solid stone which towered over the Niagara River dated back to the Silurian age of geologic shifting and depositing. Its fame derives from its location, where the river plunges into Niagara Falls. Blasting and hacking through limestone and mountainous material proved to be a daunting task. At this point, crews placed 5 locks along a 3-mile corridor to continue the canal over the escarpment.

To plow through and discard earth, horses and mules pulled a "slip scraper", a kind of bulldozer. Clay set in stone lined the inside walls and bottom of the canal. Hundreds of German mason workers laid the stonework. Schooled engineers from England, and particularly from Holland, employed their skills and expertise to literally rebuild nature. Engineers honed their techniques during construction which included the building of aqueducts to redirect water flow. One such structure measured 950-feet long in order to span 800-feet of river.

The major obstacle, however, was felling trees through virgin forests and moving the soil. Ingenuity won out when workers flung ropes up over the top branches and winched trees down. They designed a device called a "stump puller" to solve the obvious problem. Its operation, though, was quite involved.

A pair of gigantic wheels was loosely mounted on an axle and a slightly smaller wheel attached to the center of that axle. A chain hooked around the axle then to a tree stump and a rope wrapped around the center wheel which then hitched to a team of oxen. When all parts of this method were synchronized to go, the torque ripped the stumps out of the earth. Mule-drawn carts pulled away soil that had been shoveled into countless wheelbarrows. Using a scraping device and a plow, a 3-man team, with horses, mules or oxen, could clear a mile in 1 year.

Men, a combination of man and animal power, or the power of a water source provided every bit of labor expended. Increased immigration to the United States made for a more plentiful labor pool. Scottish and Irish men made up many of the workers on the Erie Canal. It is said that hundreds of them died of malaria while working in the "Montezuma Marsh" (Cayuga Lake, west of Syracuse) section of the canal, thus bringing construction to a temporary halt.

Structural challenges included leaks which randomly occurred along the length of the canal. Sealing them with hydraulic cement which hardened under water provided a solution. Before it could be repaired, erosion on the clay bottom of the canal limited speed to just 4-miles-per-hour.

A Little Short of Madness

Enlargements of the Erie Canal

The Erie Canal was enlarged twice after its initial construction and opening because merchants quickly exceeded the original estimated amount of annual tonnage permitted—1.5 million tons. From 1834 through 1862, the canal underwent its first enlargement, widening it to 70-feet and deepening it to 7-feet. Workers added other locks rebuilt them in new locations and created new aqueducts. They straightened or re-routed some sections, leaving shorter segments of the original canal of 1825 in place.

In 1903, the construction of the "Barge Canal" again enlarged the channel and consisted of the Erie Canal and the three prominent branches of the state canal system—the Champlain, the Oswego, and the Cayuga-Seneca. This work concluded in 1918, making the components of the Barge Canal network 12 to 14-feet deep, 120 to 200-feet wide, with a retained length of 363-miles from Albany to Buffalo. In addition, crews built 57 more locks to handle barges carrying up to 3,000 tons of cargo, with lifts of 6 to 40-feet. This is the present configuration of the Erie Canal which is now known as the New York State Canal System.[27]

...And the Award Goes To ?????????

So, who gets the credit for the Erie Canal? If that question came up on a history quiz, pens clamped into eager hands, would scribble the name "De Witt Clinton" as the answer. Yes, he was, indeed, the man of the hour... and of the era.

Here's another question. Who deserves the credit for the Erie Canal? There are 15 possible answers—and 13 of them are rather doubtful.

~

The New York State Canal System, or the Erie Canal as we like to remember it, is a remarkable treasure. It flows rich in history and culture, permeated by bold ideas and unfaltering spirit. Throw in powerful politics—surely, blood, sweat and tears—a good measure of vetoing and, yes, some genuine smiles.

Now, let's indulge in a bit of pure nostalgia. Folklore, stories, poems and songs emerged from the Erie Canal era, mostly from those who built it

This painting by Carl Rakeman, 1825, shows the "Seneca Chief", the flagship of a flotilla making the maiden voyage down the Erie Canal.

or worked along its 363-mile expanse. As populations grew and the canal prospered—not only as a service, but as a place and destination in and of itself—people looked to the location as a vacation spot for enjoyment and for a glimpse of other ways of life. Fifty-thousand people once depended on the Erie Canal for employment and for a way to improve their lives. An entire culture evolved around canal life.

For many, canal boats doubled as homes or floating houses, traveling from town to town. The male head of the family might have served as captain, while his wife cooked aboard their boat, tending to children and daily chores. Some youngsters even became "hoggees", walking mules or horses at a steady pace, as they pulled vessels through the canal. For others with a bit more money, packet boats were the way to travel for gambling and entertainment on the canal. Whole families often met, year-to-year, at the same locations to share stories and adventures.

Today, the canal might brag of its former glory, as pleasure crafts, fisherman, and cyclists traverse the busy towpaths of the 19th century. The

Erie Canal is a gift that keeps on giving.

Clinton's Legacy

The completion and official opening of the Erie Canal in 1825 brought about a significant change in the public's opinion of Clinton. Newspaper reporters, who previously criticized Clinton's persistence about building the canal, openly celebrated his achievement.

"The Marriage of the Waters"- A mural decoration in the DeWitt Clinton High School, New York City, showing a scene connected with the ceremony of opening the Erie Canal in 1825. - Copyright 1905, C.Y. Turner

An article in the *New Hampshire Sentinel* read: "The efforts of Gov. Clinton to advance the best interest of the State over which he presides are very generally acknowledged both by his constituents and the public abroad. His exertions in favor of the great Canal have identified his name with that noble enterprise, and he will be remembered while its benefits are experienced. Yield credit to Clinton, and hail him by name".

The official opening ceremonies began on October 25, 1825 and lasted 10 days as Clinton and his party of supporters sailed along the canal from Buffalo to Albany in a packet boat called the "Seneca Chief". Everywhere along the route, cheering crowds greeted the sailing procession. From Albany, it traveled from the mouth of Lake Erie to New York City, where, in dramatic fashion, Clinton poured 2 casks of water from Lake Erie into the Atlantic Ocean, symbolizing the first connection of waters to the east and west. This moment has been captured in numerous paintings and in books, as the "Wedding of the Waters".

The Guest of Honor

One particular individual had been invited aboard the "Seneca Chief", without whom there might not have been a celebration at all on that brisk fall day in 1825.

DeWitt Clinton believed in him, and that's all Jesse Hawley needed to know. Not only did Clinton believe in and agree with the essays of this singular writer named "Hercules"; he publicly credited Hawley as the first to conceptualize the idea of a canal system, the first to create documented plans for the Erie Canal, and as the first and sole author of them.

Hawley was chairman of the official canal celebration delegation. To further show his gratitude, Governor Clinton asked Hawley to make the first speech at the opening ceremony. This is what he said:

"New York has made the longest canal, in the least time, with the least experience, for the least money, and of the greatest public utility of any other in the world."

Jesse Hawley gained greater public recognition in 1836 when he became treasurer of his town, Lockport. He served his post until 1842, when he died in Cambria, New York, while visiting friends. Like Clinton, he had lived to see the Erie Canal become a reality.

He was buried in Cold Spring Cemetery, a short distance from the canal. A white, marble obelisk marks his resting place. It reads: "Cold Spring Cemetery –Jesse Hawley who first advocated building the Erie Canal in 1805 is buried here. Friend of DeWitt Clinton".

Not only are Hawley's writings about a proposed canal generally acknowledged for creating the waterway that turned New York into a world economic power; but also for helping to facilitate a immense movement of peoples and ideas.[28]

This would bring forth the major social, political, and religious movements of the 19th century. They changed America.

Part Three

CHANGE

Chapter 6

Salvation

The First Great Awakening (1730s-1770s), a widespread Protestant religious movement of the mid-18th century, occurred both in Europe and in the American colonies in the United States. It was characterized by the strengthening of one's personal spirituality, fostered by introspection and piety, to ultimately achieve a higher standard of individual morality. The ideology's followers hoped salvation would be granted by Christ, as a reward for living a pure spiritual life.

The movement began a "new Age of Faith" primarily in England, Scotland, and Germany. It gained popularity among followers who challenged the schools of thought born out of the Age of Enlightenment or the Age of Reason (1620s-1780s), which valued reason above religious faith, and institutions deeply rooted in social culture, such as the Roman Catholic Church.

The First Great Awakening reaffirmed the feeling that being truly religious meant trusting emotions or feelings of the heart, rather than relying only on intellect and analytical thinking.

The American awakening surfaced among Presbyterians in Pennsylvania and New Jersey, led by the Reverend William Tennent, a Scottish-Irish immigrant. Many knew Tennent for initiating religious revivals in the colonies of those states; but, he was also recognized as the first clergyman to train others to convert sinners. He named his school "the Log College", which today is known as Princeton University.

The movement also spurred missionary activity among such Native

Americans as David Brainerd, Eleazar Wheelock, and Samuel Kirkland, who were involved in early anti-slavery movements and humanitarian causes. Their work and beliefs led to the founding of several educational establishments, including Brown University, Rutgers University, and Dartmouth College in the northeast.[1]

The Second Great Awakening (1790-1840s)

The 19th century companion to its prior revival movement in the United States, the Second Great Awakening aimed at ridding society of its ills and evils, essentially in anticipation of the Second Coming of Jesus Christ.

After 1820, strong numbers of Baptist and Methodist congregations felt drawn to this spiritual renewal movement, and willingly followed preachers who championed the cause. Those wanting this increased spiritual awareness opposed skepticism (the philosophical theory that complete knowledge is impossible), deism (the view that an uninvolved God exists but does not intervene in the human realm), and rationalism (reason, not experience, is the foundation of certainty and the ultimate authority in religion). Many new denominations resulted, as well as a myriad of related reform movements.

Those who clung to and perpetuated the principles of the Second Awakening believed in a far-off but attainable certainty called millennialism. The belief that for a period of 1,000 years—prior to the final judgment (the assessment of souls after death)—Christ would reign in a Paradise on Earth ushering in the Golden Age.

The religious teachings of both the First and Second Awakenings enabled people to channel their personal spiritual futures by making efforts to eliminate the evils of mankind, in preparation for the arrival of the deity, Jesus Christ. These powerful movements would lay the ground work for history-changing events, such as the Abolitionist Movement, the pursuit of Women's Rights, and more.[2]

The Burned Over District

In the early 1820s the frontier still covered most of western New York and clergy didn't often venture out that far. Many settlers embraced versions of folk religion, which consisted of cultural and religious customs, apart from

Salvation

officially established religions and practices. Yet, the swift rise of evangelism would have a profound effect on the role of religion in one's daily life, prompting historian, Emerson Klees, to refer to this period in history and its most active locations as the "Psychic Highway". Specifically, a concentrated area from southwest Buffalo to Albany, along the route of the Erie Canal became the most prominent location for evangelism in New York State. Eager evangelists found pools of willing participants looking for salvation; many of whom were converted to Protestant sects, primarily those of the Congregationalists, the Baptists, and the Methodists.

Charles G. Finney, American Presbyterian Minister and leader during the "Second Great Awakening". Coined the phrase, "Burned Over District".

By the late 1840s, Charles Grandison Finney (known as the Father of Modern Revivalism), tirelessly devoted his efforts to the conversion of sinners. An area he managed to convert would be known as a "burned over district". He believed his goal had been so thoroughly accomplished that there would be no "fuel" left to "burn". Those who made their living through farming understood the phrase very well. A swift wildfire cannot burn crops without fuel. For Finney, his religious fire burned sin to the ground, thereby exhausting all fuel.

Born in Connecticut to farmer parents, Charles Grandison Finney (1792-1875), American Presbyterian minister and leader in the Second Great Awakening, moved with his family to Henderson, New York, in Jefferson County, after the Revolutionary War.

The youngest of 15 children, Finney grew to an imposing figure at 6-foot 3-inches tall, with a piercing gaze that regularly captured the attention of many when he attended lively revival meetings with his family. He never went to college, but "read the law", and studied as a lawyer's apprentice, when he experienced a dramatic, life-changing religious experience.

On a day like any other, an unassuming Finney experienced a mighty "baptism with the Holy Spirit or the Spirit of God", an event associated with the bestowal of spiritual gifts, including the empowerment to lead a Christian Ministry.

In 1821, he began studying with Presbyterian minister, George Washington Gale, under whose tutelage Finney learned the principles—and dynamics—of Christian ministering. He also developed his own innovative, powerful preaching style. He could be seen actively moving about and delivering his messages in extemporaneous fashion (knowing and delivering the message well enough without referring to a strict written outline). He also gained notoriety by being among the first preachers to allow women to pray out loud in public meetings, to allow "potential Christians" to occupy the "anxious seat", a place to ponder religion and receive prayer, and to publicly censure individuals by name in his sermons.

In 1832, he became minister of the Chatham Street Chapel in New York City, and founded with Lewis Tappan, the Broadway Tabernacle, a Congregationalist church on Manhattan's upper west side at 93rd Street. Today, it is the Broadway United Church of Christ.

In 1835, he became a professor at Oberlin College in Ohio. More than ten years later, he was appointed as its second president, serving until 1866. Oberlin College became the first American college to accept women and African-American students. College faculty and student groups actively participated in the abolitionist movement and shared in bi-racial efforts to help fugitive slaves traveling within the nation's Underground Railroad system.

Finney is the author of *Religious Revivals*, a definitive work which emphasizes the importance of individual will in one's salvation. He married 3 times and each wife both accompanied and supported him on his revival tours. He originated many of the methods used by such famous revivalists as Dwight Lyman Moody (1837-1899), John Wilbur Chapman (1859-1918), and William Miller (1782-1849). Modern-day evangelists like Billy Sunday (William Ashley Sunday) and Billy Graham have adopted the approaches of these predecessors. It has been said of Finney that "evangelism entered modernity with him."[3]

~

Salvation

The Erie Canal, praised by many as the 8th Wonder of the World, more than accomplished its primary purpose: to enhance the economy of New York State via the network of major city ports along the east coast, and into the growing west. Jesse Hawley—and the string of canal visionaries before him—would be proud and probably nod their heads in agreeable "I-told-you-so" fashion.

Many also clearly realized the social and cultural benefits of the canal almost immediately upon its completion and early operation. European settlers, mostly Irish and German, and Canadians, soon expanded populations of Indian settlements all available for employment in and around the canal and for new business establishments. Those who traveled for pleasure also contributed to the success of this magnificent purpose for a waterway. The transfer of cultural nuances and intellectual ideas became just as valuable and noteworthy as the quality (and cost) to ship and receive goods and every manner of cargo.

The Erie Canal even facilitated New York State's religious rebirth—which soon spread west. This superb piece of transportation genius literally brought those dispensing salvation to the very people who wanted to be saved. This sweeping, unparalleled magnitude of evangelism would have a profound effect on society—and history.[4]

There's Gold in the Hills

Joseph Smith (1805-1844), founder of the Mormon religion, claimed he discovered a set of golden plates in Hill Cumorah (also known as Mormon Hill, Gold Bible Hill and Inspiration Point) in Manchester, New York, in 1822 or 1823. "On the west side of this hill, not far from the top, under a stone of considerable size, lay the plates, deposited in a stone box", wrote Smith.

He claimed an angel named "Moroni", who visited Smith in the same location on September 22 of each year between 1823 and 1827, gave him the "plates" (a series of books). The inscribed messages on the plates became the content of the Book of Mormon, the earliest sacred text of the Latter Day Saint movement, first published in 1830 by Joseph Smith as the Book of Mormon: An Account Written by the Hand of Mormon Upon Plates Taken from the Plates of Nephi. [5]

Mormon belief asserts that the Book of Mormon contains writings of ancient prophets who lived on the American continent from approximately 2200 B.C. to 421 A.D. Nephi or the Nephites are one of four groups (with

Joseph Smith, founder of the Mormon Church. He was 24 when he published the Book of Mormon.

the Lamanites, the Jaredites, and the Mulekites) to have settled in the ancient Americas and are mentioned throughout the Book of Mormon to describe their religious, political, and cultural traditions. The Book of Mormon is regarded primarily as scripture and secondly, as a historical record of God's hand in the lives of the ancient inhabitants of the Americas. Followers of the Book of Mormon became known as Mormons, Latter Day Saints, or simply, Saints.

Smith wrote that the unknown characters inscribed on the plates had been written in "reformed Egyptian" by the last Mormon prophet to do so. That individual, the mortal man Moroni, then buried the plates in the New York hills and later, after this death, appeared to Smith as an angel.[6]

He instructed Smith to have the writings translated into English and to use the resulting books to restore Christ's "true church" in the "latter days". The term "latter day" distinguishes biblical saints from modern saints who live in the latter days, or until the end of days/end of time before the Second Coming of Christ.

Salvation

Smith began this primitive Christian movement by founding the Church of Christ, which joined the plethora of revivalist efforts in New York during the Second Great Awakening. The movement's first converts felt drawn to Smith's account of finding the plates in the New York hills. He told them his ability to translate—by looking into a "seer stone" placed in a stovepipe hat—was given "by the gift and power of God." In 1829, Smith and an associate, Oliver Cowdery, began baptizing new converts into the Church of Christ. Smith's followers saw and revered him as a modern-day prophet.

Mormons view life on earth as a temporary state in which humans are tested, but gain valuable moral experiences that will serve them well after their physical death on earth and move to the next step in God's plan. They believe their mortal existence is part of an ancient, pre-life history with their Heavenly Father which progresses, as such, in their earthly lives.

When Smith attempted to have copies of the Book of Mormon printed, several printers refused including E.B. Grandin, Jonathan Hadley of Palmyra, New York, who also published the anti-Masonic *Palmyra Freeman*, and Thurlow Weed of Rochester. Finally, Elihu F. Marshall, Weed's competitor in Rochester, consented to publish the book.

At the same time, various area newspapers ran critical articles on the Book of Mormon. The *Wayne Sentinel* published just the book's title page in 1829. Jonathan Hadley's anti-Mormon article, originally printed in the *Palmyra Freeman*, was reprinted in publications in Lockport, New York; Salem, Massachusetts; and Plainville, Ohio. A number of Rochester papers also satirized the written style of the Book of Mormon, calling it "Biblical sounding".

Amid these unpopular sentiments and personal financial troubles, Smith and his wife moved to Harmony, Pennsylvania. Martin Harris, friend and landowner, offered those help. Harris and Smith approached E.B. Grandin again, hoping to negotiate a more lucrative deal than the one offered by publisher Elihu Marshall. They held negotiations with Grandin from July to August of 1829, using Harris' land holdings as collateral.

Grandin entered into a secured transaction, agreeing to print 5,000 copies of the Book of Mormon for $3,000 to be paid within 18 months after printing began. Harris would pay half of this amount; the other half would be paid by Smith and his brother, Hyrum. Smith and his wife had already moved to Harmony. Before leaving New York, Smith reported having a revelation that the original manuscript of the Book of Mormon should remain in his home, while his friend, Oliver Cowdery, would transcribe parts of the text and Hyrum—accompanied by a guard—would carry each day's transcript to Grandin's office for typesetting.

Smith was unsuccessful in raising his $1,500 share of printing costs. During this time, he sent Cowdery to Toronto as a "missionary", to try to raise funds and perhaps secure a Canadian copyright for the book. In 1830, Hyrum Smith and Cowdery discovered that Abner Cole, newspaper publisher of the *Reflector* in Palmyra, had begun printing portions of the Book of Mormon—at Grandin's printing shop. Smith turned the matter over to an arbitrator who deemed Cole's publication as a copyright infringement, ordering him to stop.

Citizens in Palmyra, however, started boycotting the printing of the Book of Mormon. Because of this, Grandin simply stopped printing. Unfortunately, Martin Harris realized then that the full cost of printing would be left to him and not shared. Angered, he approached Smith, who placated him by entering into a payment contract with him—and Grandin resumed printing.

As the first copies of the book became available for sale, Harris—who had agreed to help sell them—had no buyers. He reconsidered his part in paying printing costs. In response, Smith cited his revelation commanding Harris, "upon penalty of eternal damnation... to impart a portion of thy property; yea, even a part of thy lands and all save the support of thy family, pay the printer's debt." Harris complied. Grandin printed copies of the Book of Mormon, and put them available for sale on the ground floor of his bookshop.[7]

Smith moved his church to Kirtland, Ohio in 1838, changing its name to the Church of Jesus Christ of Latter Day Saints. From there, he moved to Far West, Missouri (1838-1839), attempting to build a "new Zion"; and to Nauvoo, Illinois, from 1839-1844. After his death, Brigham Young, who brought Mormonism to Utah, succeeded him. As of 2013, the Church of Jesus Christ of Latter Day Saints has over 15 million members.

The Millerites: Look to 1843!

Farmer, sheriff, justice of the peace and Baptist preacher, William Miller (1782-1849), is credited with the founding of the religious movement known as the Millerites, which would later morph into the Advent Christian Church (1861) and the much larger group, the Seventh Day Adventists (1863). This group observes the Sabbath on Saturday, the 7th day of the week. Miller's revival movement was yet another piece of the ambitious religious resurgence puzzle played out in New York's Burned Over District.

William Miller was born in Pittsfield, Massachusetts, to Captain William Miller, a veteran of the American Revolution, and Paulina Phelps Miller. At 4-years-old his family moved to rural Low Hampton, New York. His mother predominately home educated by him, and he attended school only for 3 months each winter between the ages of 9 and 14.

As a young man, he read with voracity and began to lean toward Deism, the belief that God made the world, but left it to people to reason

William Miller, Baptist preacher credited with establishing religious movement known as the "Millerites" which became the Seventh-Day Adventist Church.

and observe the natural world to determine the existence of a creator. After volunteering for service in the War of 1812, Miller concluded he had evidenced the presence of God in the plight of humans, and began a systematic study of the Bible to find clarification to his spiritual questions.

He adapted his beliefs from the prophecies of Daniel—particularly Daniel 8—and Revelation, which spoke of Christ's return to earth. He took to preaching in smaller towns first, and then moved to larger cities where crowds of ministers and laymen joined him. In 1833, Miller announced his belief that the Second Advent of Jesus Christ would occur around the year 1843, but ultimately by the spring of 1844. He finalized the date, by some means, to be October 22, 1844.

Miller relied most upon what he interpreted the symbolic meanings of Daniel's prophecies to be, especially Daniel 8:14: "He said to me, 'It will take 2,300 evenings and mornings; then the sanctuary will be reconsecrated.' "

Using the Year-Day principle (a method of interpretation in Bible prophecy in which the word "day" is symbolic for the word "year" in actual time) Miller calculated that the 2,300 day period began in 457 BC, culminating in 1843, his predicted year for the Second Coming of Christ.

Yet, October 22, 1844 came and passed amid religious frenzy and heated anticipation; but, Christ did not make his physical appearance. The date became known as the Great Disappointment and was recorded as Miller's first public failure. Adventist pioneer, Hiram Edson, wrote of the day, ""Our fondest hopes and expectations were blasted, and such a spirit of weeping came over us as I never experienced before... we wept, and wept, till the day dawn."

Still, Miller clung to the concept of Christ's Second Coming. He said, "The year of expectation was according to prophecy; but... there might be an error in Bible chronology, which was of human origin, that could throw the date off somewhat and account for the discrepancy." His faith remained strong, as he continued, "Although I have been twice disappointed, I am not yet cast down or discouraged. . . . I have fixed my mind upon another time, and here I mean to stand until God gives me more light—and that is Today, TODAY, and TODAY, until He comes, and I see Him for whom my soul yearns."[8]

Despite its major setbacks, from 1840 on, Millerism grew into a national movement. Joshua Vaughn Himes, pastor of the Chardon Street Chapel in Boston and also an experienced publisher, wasn't completely convinced of Miller's claims; but, he began the paper *Signs of the Times* which publicized them. This continues to be published today under the same name as a monthly magazine by the Seventh-Day Adventist Church.[9]

The Temperance Movement

Temperance—as in drinking less and/or in showing more self-restraint in the face of temptation or desire—implies the same kinds of avid warnings against drunken behavior as revivalist sects put forth about living sinful lives.

The Temperance Movement was a natural addition to the panoply of religious revival movements in New York and the country, especially at the time of the Second Great Awakening. The thrust of the temperance movement fell in perfectly with religious messages that appealed to the concept of individual choice and responsibility.[10]

Americans drank in excess after the Revolutionary War. It was a way of life. Consumption eased the effects of hard physical labor. Many also used it as payment for jobs well done. The presence of alcohol had become synonymous with social functions, from weddings to the gatherings of military personnel. Overall, with water often being contaminated, many found drinking fermented and distilled beverages to be safer.

Beginning in the 1800s, movements to induce more temperate drinking or drinking less, took hold. By the 1820s, the message blossomed into an appeal for total abstinence from alcohol. Such initiatives linked religious and social reform in a variety of important ways, including humanitarian awareness for the care of the mentally ill, the treatment of prisoners, the rights of women, and ways to end slavery.

Temperance associations were formally established in New York and in Massachusetts, including the interdenominational American Society for the Promotion of Temperance, founded in Boston in 1826. By the mid 1830s, similar groups had organized in other states.

Women who, along with their children, had endured the brutal effects of drunkenness at the hands of husbands and father achieved temperance efforts in the 19th and early 20th century. Many people blamed alcohol for many of society's ills, including poor health, destitution and crime.[11]

The Shakers

They did not tremble in fear or nervously cower. Rather, the Shakers were described as being "ecstatic" in their worship of God. They joyfully "shook", moved rhythmically, or appeared to be dancing as they prayed as a reaction to receiving spiritual messages of faith from God during religious revival services. With this, they chose to express their relationship with the deity and to partake in their salvation.

The Shakers sect (originally known as the United Society of Believers in Christ's Second Appearing) came out of the Quaker religion. Critics named them the "Quaking Shakers". As charismatic Christians, Shakers believed in the work of the Holy Spirit, spiritual "gifts" or graces given by the Holy Spirit, and the existence of every day miracles. They practiced pacifism and supported equality of the sexes. They lived in simple, sparse surroundings. By the late 1700s, the Shakers had become one of the strongest surviving "new religions" born out of the Burned Over District era, with communities throughout Maine, New England, New York, Ohio and Kentucky.

Shakers were known as "Shaking Quakers", due to their ecstatic behavior during worship services.

Founded in 1774 by Englishwoman Ann Lee (1736-1784), the Shaker religion hinged on 4 rules: communal living, celibacy, the confession of sins, and the desire to live separate and apart from the outside world.

Lee came from a poor background. She never learned to read or write and circumstances forced her to work in her youth. She entered into an unhappy marriage and gave birth to 4 children, none of whom lived beyond their early years.

She began to experience "visions" containing life truths, as to "the odiousness of sin" (in particular, sexual relations) and "the depravity of human nature". In 1758, James and Jane Wardley, followers of French evangelists who had escaped to England to avoid religious persecution in France, converted her to Quakerism. As a member of the Wardleys' small group, she began to preach on the subject of "man's fall from grace". The Church of England considered her a dissident and ordered her to be sent to jail in 1770. Finally, in 1774 she and her husband and several relatives and followers sailed for New York. In New York City, the group split. Some traveled up the Hudson River to Niskayuna (Watervliet today) outside of Albany. Lee remained in the city for

Salvation

a time, but left for Niskayuna when her husband deserted her. Friends in the New York State community prepared a refuge for her.

They located their community, however, on the edge of frontier land, far away from any possibility of enticing converts to the Shaker religion. In 1779, the community moved to New Lebanon, near the New York/Massachusetts border. There, the group experienced revivals of the New Light Baptists. A number of new converts to this group felt unsatisfied with their methods of worship and appealed to "Mother Ann" to join her community. Through 1780 and 1784, Lee ushered in new believers and founded other small Shaker colonies in Maine, New Hampshire, Massachusetts, and Connecticut. In 1784, Ann Lee passed away, leaving a doctrine advising chastity, humility, and temperance.

In 1824, Ohio Shaker, Richard Pelham, visited his brother, Joseph, in Lyons, New York, convincing him that the Shaker way of life would answer his spiritual yearnings. Joseph agreed and later became the leader of his own community at Sodus Bay at Lake Ontario, a place rich in farmland and timber. Eventually, money was appropriated privately and by other Shaker communities in New England to enlarge the compound at Sodus Bay by a generous 1,331 acres.

By 1831, the members had built more barns, farm houses, a grist mill, and a meeting house. This complex, however, would be threatened by the Sodus Canal Company, hired by New York State to construct a canal right through Shaker land. In 1836, the community sold the land and purchased another site in Groveland, New York, their new home. Between 1855 and 1870, the nation's economy became more industrialized, interrupting the serenity and simplicity of Shaker life and membership in Groveland declined drastically.

In time, Groveland succumbed to the ravages of weather, which destroyed farmland with harsh intermittent dry and wet spells, as well as being occasionally flooded by the Genesee River. Recurrent natural wild fires also damaged living quarters and the grist mill. By 1887, Groveland found itself in unrecoverable debt, with only 34 members living on the premises. They made the decision to close the community and sell its buildings and lands to the state of New York, which ultimately transferred them to the New York State Department of Corrections.[12]

~

The Shaker life was one of work and prayer. They followed the motto "Hands to work, hearts to God". It's truly ironic that prison cell bars, fences, barbed wire, observation towers, and flood lights now stand on what once housed the peaceful, pristine retreat for religious worshipers who happily lived apart from others.

True freedom can mean different things to different people. Prison inmates have forfeited it. The Shakers and the many followers of the new religions, believed in the promise and power of personal salvation, and then became the vanguard for great social movements leading to freedom for millions.

Chapter 7

Without Struggle There's No Progress

"Believe in yourself."
"Take advantage of every opportunity."
"Use the power of the spoken and written language to effect
positive change for yourself and society."

~ Frederick Douglass

One of the most complex, dramatic stories of life as a slave belongs to Frederick Douglass (1818-1895)—an iconic figure in America's Abolitionist Movement—and perhaps in the history of western New York.

An Extraordinary Life

Frederick Augustus Washington Bailey, the man we know as Frederick Douglass, was born into slavery at Holme Hill Farm in Easton, Maryland in 1817... or maybe 1818.

Most slaves never knew their exact birth dates, except to maybe hear others speak of the fall time, or spring time, to refer to the birth of a new child. The law protected slaveholders and demanded the children of slave women to "follow (in the) condition of their mothers", even though they systematically removed children from their mothers, sometimes as infants. The children would then be assigned to

Frederick Douglass- social reformer, abolitionist, orator, writer, and statesman. Moved to Rochester, New York in 1847 to begin his career as newspaper publisher.

an older slave woman who could no longer do field work. A child could never bond with its natural mother, or with its unnatural, grandmother-like replacement. Douglass knew his mother's name to be Harriet Bailey and came to believe his father was a white man, most probably, his master. But, he dared not ask.

Each slave had a name, to which they answered, but it did not engender self-worth. They lacked personal history, crucial points of life references, and hope. Nothing but a cruel wasteland of the mind and heart defined them. Even children—clad only in coarse muslin shirts barely covering their knees—worked as hard as adults until their muscles burned, only to crawl into a discarded corn sack at day's end and sleep the night on a cold cement floor.[1]

Douglass wrote in his autobiography, "My feet have so cracked with frost that the pen with which I am writing might be laid in the gashes".

The notion that slaves sang out of happiness as they toiled, couldn't be more flawed. They vocalized rhythmic sounds out of sheer despair, hoping that the Lord above would hear their pleas and rescue them.

"Slaves sing most when they are most unhappy. The songs of the slave represent the sorrows of his heart; and he is relieved by them, only as an aching heart is relieved by its tears. Crying for joy, and singing for joy, were alike uncommon to me while in the jaws of slavery. To the songs I trace my first glimmering conception of the dehumanizing character of slavery".[2]

Little did Douglass know that a man-made waterway, conceived as an alternate way to transport goods, would also transport human cargo and in the process, change America.

The Erie Canal and the Underground Railroad

The Erie Canal (1825) was the greatest boon to travel between the Atlantic seaboard and the Great Lakes, facilitating unprecedented economic development and the proliferation of social communication. It also became a prominent means of transportation for American fugitive slaves escaping to the north and Canada.

The key locations of other New York State canals connecting to the Erie—Champlain, Oswego and the Cayuga-Seneca—also claim equal responsibility for turning unimaginable journeys into realities for escaping slaves. They also helped grow the numbers of anti-slavery and women's suffrage leaders and supporters in the mid-1800s.

Without Struggle There's No Progress

Another path called the Underground Railroad—did provide the road to freedom at a much more costly price. While not an actual railroad, the carefully planned process of transporting fugitive slaves incorporated the terms used during a railroad journey or transfer of a shipment. As soon as an escaping slave made contact with a friend, sympathizer or known helper, he/she officially became a traveling entity in the "Underground Railroad".

Organizers called the routes between safe houses, lines. These distances spanned around 15 miles long, but shortened considerably as the route progressed further north. They called the stopping places or homes, stations. Those individuals who aided the process were called conductors. To insure as much secrecy as possible, fugitive slaves were called packages or freight. "Checkers" or "brakemen" methodically scanned the area, before and after "freight" was added or taken from the run.

It comes as no surprise that Frederick Douglass' home in Rochester, New York, would become one of the most critical and final stops for slaves escaping into Canada. Douglass, in fact, went by "conductor" at his stop. The homes of people who shared this designation had added some manner of false walls, cubbies, closets, and storage areas, all built to maintain a semblance of everyday architecture and fixtures—not spaces for human shelter.

New York State's Underground Railroad links were best served by their proximity to travel by rail or water. New York's major cities developed along the canal corridor. By mid-century, 80% of the population of New York lived within 25 miles of the state's canals. Rochester was one of those pivotal cities. Rochester grew up and around the Erie Canal, which originally ran straight through the middle of the city, crossing the Genesee River by an aqueduct. When the new aqueduct began leaking, New York State replaced it in 1842, as they widened the canal.[3]

Canal Villages

New York's canals offered outright escape routes for fugitive slaves. Some of these encounters have been recorded.

For example, in 1834, Moses Roper escaped from Savannah, Georgia, and signed on for work on an Erie Canal boat heading west. At Albany, he boarded a Champlain Canal boat, which carried him to Vermont.

In August of 1841, Elizabeth Smith Miller—daughter of Gerrit Smith, the abolitionist who helped Douglass publish his newspaper—sailed with her mother on one of the canals. Their final destination would be Rochester. "When Mother left the cabin she found a fugitive slave woman on board with her little boy, two-years-old—we gave her 10 shillings. At the landing, we took a coach for Rochester. Farewell—Gold bless you," she wrote.

In the same year, William Clarke—a European American Underground Railroad agent—arranged travel for slaves from Syracuse to Oswego via the Oswego Canal. "There were three fugitives shipped on board the old line of packets this morning for Oswego," he wrote.

Also in 1841, New York State passed a law ruling that anyone accused of being fugitives from slavery were considered free as soon as they crossed the New York State line. In a gesture of compassion, Edwin W. Clarke, cousin to William Clarke and also an Underground Railroad agent boarded a boat en route to Oswego by the Oswego Canal to inform a young African American woman and her 2 companions that, according to New York State law, she now held the title of a free woman.

Canal Villages and Fugitive Slaves

The opening of the Erie Canal in 1825 was a timely preface to the abolition of slavery in New York State in 1827. Canal villages sprung up from business and social communities that settled on or near the canals. These ideal locations provided temporary places for people escaping from slavery.

In the late 1820s and early 1830s, free blacks began to move to canal cities, finding work as laborers, boatmen, hotel workers, or barbers—a particularly advantageous trade at the time.

While it still seems true that all neighborhood news—personal or otherwise—is filtered through America's barbershops or beauty salons, the African American barber was a unique professional, serving a diversified European American clientele. Port and canal cities hosted the likes of Canadian captains, sailors, and a good number of United States citizens, in various jobs. This climate allowed barbers to hear customers' feelings about slavery and abolition. Who sympathized? Who was a pursuer?

Information that might be useful in planning a slave's passage through the Underground Railroad wove through networks of canal families, churches, schools, businesses, and barbershops.

Without Struggle There's No Progress

Canal Villages and Safe Houses

Canal villages provided locations for safe houses in the Underground Railroad in New York simply because of the immense geographical areas they covered.

3 main Underground Railroad Routes intersected New York State:

- The first and major route ran directly north, from New York City, to Albany; it then ran north again along the Champlain Canal and onto Lake Champlain to Canada.

- The second route headed west from Albany—through Utica, Syracuse, Rochester, and Buffalo—with secondary routes leading to Canada along the Oswego Canal and Lake Ontario ports at Pultneyville, Charlotte (near Rochester) and other western locations.

- The third route began on land from southeastern Pennsylvania, north to the Finger Lakes and then either west to Lake Erie (through Elmira) or north along the Finger Lakes' intersection with the Albany-to-Buffalo route.

Every major city along the canal corridor embraced a network of Underground Railroad supporters, both African American and European American. In his last autobiography, *Life and Times of Frederick Douglass* (1892), he noted the original route he traveled to freedom: Baltimore, Maryland; to Wilmington, Delaware; north to Philadelphia, north to New York City and Albany, then west to Syracuse and Rochester.

In the 1830s and 1840s growing numbers of abolitionist groups raised money, donated clothing, provided and/or paid for transportation, and arranged work for slaves in the Underground Railroad.[4]

The Message and the Motto

By 1843, Douglass was completely immersed in his anti-slave mission as preacher, orator, and abolitionist, sharing his story as a recognized national speaker. However, when his first autobiography, the *Narrative of the Life of Frederick Douglass, an American Slave*, was published in 1845, Douglass and his wife, Anna, moved to London, England, for 2 years, still fearing that he might be captured and returned to slavery. The book gave precise information;

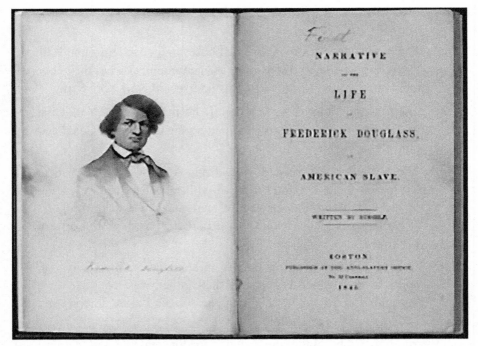

including names, places, dates, and all the life events he endured as a slave. (See Appendix D)

In 1846, friends and supporters in London raised over $700 to purchase Douglass' freedom from Thomas Auld, Jr., finally and officially making him a free man. Douglass returned to the United States in 1847 and chose to settle in the city of Rochester, New York, which had began to attract national attention as a hub of support for abolitionism and the woman's suffrage movement.

Susan B. Anthony, the president of the National American Woman Suffrage Association and also a resident of Rochester, became a friend of Douglass and supporter of anti-slavery efforts. He was, in fact, the only male speaker who attended the National Women's Rights Convention in 1848 near Seneca Falls.

In his speech at the convention, he stressed the similarities between the plights of black men and American women, both of whom had been treated as inferior entities and thus, denied the right the vote.[5]

Anthony, raised as a Quaker, and Douglass formed a lifelong friendship. After Douglass attended the first Women's Rights Convention in Seneca Falls,

Without Struggle There's No Progress

he published his thoughts about it in his newspaper, the *North Star*:

> "All that distinguishes man as an intelligent and accountable being, is equally true of woman; and if that government is only just which governs by the free consent of the governed, there can be no reason in the world for denying to woman the exercise of the elective franchise, or a hand in making and administering the laws of the land."

Recalling Douglass' presence at the convention, Anthony said, "From that day until the day of his death Frederick Douglass was an honorary member of the National Women's Suffrage Association. In all our conventions, he was the honored guest who sat on our platform and spoke in our gatherings."[6] Douglass died in 1895, only hours after sitting next to Anthony at a meeting held in Washington, D.C.

During this time support for the anti-slavery and women's rights movements overlapped. This occasion in history marked when individuals rose up to voice their core beliefs, assert religious and political preferences, and support issues that elevated the importance of the individual and one's basic human rights. Much of it played out in Rochester.[6]

Off West Main Street, and west of Rochester's downtown area, sits a park close to Anthony's original home on Madison Street. The home is now the National Susan B. Anthony Museum and House. The park's focal point is a 2001 bronzed sculpture by Pepsy Kettavong called "Let's Have Tea". It portrays Anthony and Douglass, sitting across from each other at a table set with a teapot, 2 cups and 2 books. The statue depicts them in the early days of their friendship, when they talked about the causes that drew them together.

The *North Star*

Douglass decided to publish his own newspaper called the *North Star* (1847-1851), taking its name from the North Star in the night sky, which escaping slaves traditionally used as a compass in their clandestine journeys to freedom.

His first edition printed on December 3, 1847, in the basement of the Memorial African Methodist Episcopal Zion church, which had become a center for underground activities in Rochester. Funds Douglass earned during speaking tours in Great Britain and Ireland absorbed the printing and publishing costs. Many consider the *North Star* to be one of the most influential African

American antislavery publications in the pre-Civil War era. People read it in the United States, Europe, and the West Indies. Its motto was, "Right is of no sex—Truth is of no color—God is the Father of us all, and we are brethren."

Martin R. Delaney and William Cooper Nell (co-editors of the newspaper) also moved to Rochester to work with Douglass. Initially, not everyone in Rochester liked the idea that their city accommodated a black newspaper. Articles in the *New York Herald* actually encouraged Rochester's citizens to confiscate the printing press and fling it into Lake Ontario. This unsettled social climate resulted in having the Douglass children, Rosetta (1839-1906), Lewis Henry (1840-1908), Frederick, Jr. (1842-1892), and Charles Remond (1844-1920), who was just 4-years old at the time, educated in another town. The last child, Annie, born in 1849, died in 1860.

Gradually, the city of Rochester—which would become known for its opposition to slavery—accepted the bold editor of the *North Star*, praising his initiative in creating a publication of his own. Many applauded his speaking talents, even when his arguments with fellow black activists became uncomfortably heated. Undeniably, Douglass' presence in the abolitionist movement in Rochester, across the northern states and even in Europe, attracted serious supporters, placing him at the center of historical events that would profoundly affect America.

In the paper's 1st issue, Douglass explained his reasons for establishing a purely African American-owned newspaper as simple, dignified common sense. He believed those who suffered injustices needed a publication of their own in which to address and share their experiences. Groups of contributors included authors, editors, and orators, alike. The creation of the *North Star*, however, put him at odds with his friend and colleague, William Lloyd Garrison, publisher of the *Liberator*.[7]

In 1851, Douglass and Garrison parted ways in disagreement about the need for a separate, black-oriented press. Garrison and Douglass also had differing opinions about the possible use of public violence to protest and end slavery. Unfortunately, the *North Star* did not enjoy the kind of financial success Douglass predicted. He earned money lecturing and even mortgaged his home in 1848 to cover the basic expenses of publishing the paper. Gerrit Smith came to his rescue.

A major 19th century figure, Gerrit Smith (1797-1874) contributed his time, energy, and money to important social causes. Additionally, he was a staunch abolitionist and supporter of the women's suffrage movement. He also published the *Liberty Party Paper*. [8]

To ease Douglass' financial struggles and to aid him in continuing to provide a public platform for abolitionism, Smith allowed the *North Star* to merge with the *Liberty Paper*, calling the new, blended publication *Frederick Douglass' Paper*.

However, in 1859, prior to departing for Europe for a previously scheduled speaking tour, Douglass permanently ceased publication.

John Brown and the Raid on Harper's Ferry (1859): "Here We Separated".

Gerrit Smith was a leading abolitionist, politician, and philanthropist. He was a member of the "Secret Six" which financially supported John Browns radical raid on Harpers Ferry.

Although Douglass had been ruminating over the use of violence in the abolitionist movement, his definitive response when informed of a planned opportunity to do so was a resounding "NO!"

Douglass first met with John Brown (1800-1859) in Springfield, Massachusetts at his home in 1848. During this meeting, Brown shared his ambitious plans to free the slaves and for the next 11 years, Brown looked to Douglass for counsel and support.

On his visit to Douglass' Rochester home in 1858, Brown spoke again of his plan to stage an armed slave revolt. Naturally, Douglass supported Brown in his desire and efforts to help escaping slaves, but did not condone or encourage the use of violence to accomplish it.

In 1859, the men met again for the last time. Brown announced the details of his plan to stage a surprise assault on the Harper's Ferry Armory in Virginia. He wanted this to be the first step in a lofty strategy to establish an independent cadre of free blacks in the mountains of Maryland and Virginia. This initiative garnered moral and financial support from many prominent Northerners.

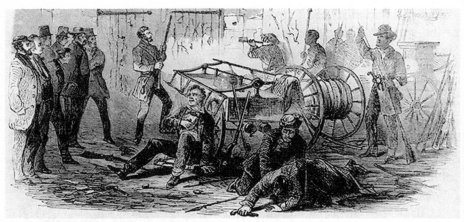

John Brown's raid on Harper's Ferry in 1859 was an attempt by Brown to start an armed slave revolt by seizing a United States arsenal. During the raid Brown was wounded, captured, and subsequently hanged for treason.

Brown intended to capture 100,000 guns and rifles, "free the slaves", and "start a war".

It's safe to say that absolutely no one wanted to free the slaves more than Frederick Douglass. He defended Brown's ideals, while denying the claims of many that the man was out of his mind. Yet, he did use the momentum of Brown's zeal to lobby President Lincoln's newly formed Republican Party and later, after the raid, launched criticisms against the President for moving slowly in support of abolitionism.[9]

Douglass advised Brown that the attack would be a "fatal mistake" and refused to consent to it or join the group. He wisely sensed the deadly potential of Brown's determination and the likelihood of its failure. He made vigorous efforts to dissuade African American men from participating in Brown's plan.

"Here we separated; he to go to Harper's Ferry, I to Rochester [New York]", wrote Douglass in his final autobiography, the *Life and Times of Frederick Douglass*.

Using the name "Isaac Smith", Brown led his meager militia of 21 men—6 whites, 5 blacks, 3 free blacks, 1 freed slave, and 1 fugitive slave, ranging in age from 21 to 49—to Harper's Ferry on July 3, 1859. He remained in a Maryland farmhouse he had previously rented; anticipating the arrival of more recruits, but none arrived.

Nonetheless, the attack ensued. The men cut the telegraph wires, captured the armory, and rounded up hostages. However, the townspeople took "potshots" at them for sport until state and federal troops arrived, including the Marines, under Robert E. Lee.

Troops quashed the raid in less than 2 days. Seventeen men perished. Brown and 6 other survivors were hanged after his trial. Many considered him a martyr and many others criticized him in anti-slavery circles. Slaveholders in the south feared that the raid might embolden their slaves to revolt, as well.

Upon Brown's arrest, authorities found and confiscated letters from Douglass among his possessions. Although he did not support Brown's plans and did not participate in the attack, Douglass concluded that since he had knowledge of the raid, he would be considered part of its conspiracy and would most likely be arrested. He also knew he would never receive a fair trial. He headed for Canada, then to Europe, to fulfill the scheduled requirements of his speaking tour. He remained abroad for 6 months.

~

John Brown's heart might have been in the right place, but he failed to see the far reaching, divisive effects of his actions. He was born in Connecticut into a deeply religious family of Calvinist Christian beliefs. At just 12-years-old, he witnessed the beating, with a shovel, of a young slave; this incident may have prompted his anti-slavery efforts to help fugitive slaves escape, especially to Canada.

Following the death of his friend, Elijah Lovejoy—a Presbyterian minister, newspaper editor, and abolitionist—Brown became more passionate about supporting anti-slavery activities and about the methods he would use in the process. A pro-slavery mob murdered Lovejoy in his Alton, Illinois warehouse, where they also destroyed his press and abolitionist materials.

Afterwards, Brown stood up in church and announced out loud, "Here before God, I consecrate my life to the destruction of slavery."

If we asked John Brown today why he opted for violence to end an institution largely predicated on physical brutality, he would most likely look at us in disbelief and toss out the benefits of our senseless psycho-babble. People who are this passionate about injustice are sometimes doomed to mimic it.

During his trial, Brown told the court that he hoped to carry out his plan, "without the snapping of a gun on either side." Even in hindsight, how can the same organizer of a military insurrection talk about his dismay over weapons being fired, when using violence to bring about freedom for slaves became his unfailing mantra? And, this wasn't his first act of aggression.

In 1856, Brown and his sons attacked pro-slavery settlers in Kansas. They physically carried 5 men from their homes, brutally beat them, finally killed them, and decapitated them. Later, Brown traveled from state to state in an effort to raise money and gather guns to conduct a war against injustice in the South.

Public opinion in the nation was clearly divided over Brown's raid on Harper's Ferry and over his vision to end slavery by killing innocent civilians. Some saw him as a hero; others saw only a crazed villain. People on both sides of the issue, however, denounced his use of violence.[10]

Gerrit Smith: Abolitionist

Gerrit Smith, a strong New York State abolitionist and social reformer, also involved himself in the women's movement and temperance groups. In Peterboro, New York, he founded his own church, "the Religion of Reason". Smith also ran for President of the United States in 1848, 1856, and 1860, but remained a Congressman from 1853–1854.

A plethora of newspaper stories swirled around Smith's knowledge of and participation in the Harper's Ferry raid. Like Brown, Smith believed in the use of violence to achieve and enforce the freedom of slaves. Unlike Brown, Smith had the financial means to accomplish it. A group of wealthy men, known as the "Secret Six", joined him and collectively backed Brown's raid on Harper's Ferry. In addition to Smith, the group consisted of Thomas Wentworth Higginson, Samuel Gridley Howe, Theodore Parker, Franklin Benjamin Sanborn, and George Luther Stearns.

In reality, only 2 of the men (Smith and Sterns) had a lot of money. Parker and Higginson worked as Unitarian ministers; Howe was a doctor, a profession considered "middle class" at the time; and, Sanborn was a teacher. These 4 felt their positions of social influence could enable them to sway others to their cause.

Gerrit Smith and John Brown knew each other for more than 10 years before the raid on Harper's Ferry.

Without Struggle There's No Progress

Acres in the Adirondacks and "Common Ground"

In 1848, Brown traveled to Peterboro because he heard of Smith's Adirondack land grants to poor black families. He proposed to Smith his desire to move his family to such land and assist the black settlers in establishing farm communities.

Smith gave away an average of 40 acres of land in northern New York to more than 2,000 poor black (and "temperate") men, attempting to aid them in meeting the land requirements for voting and to establish self-sufficiency. He gave land to poor whites, as well. For women, however, Smith deemed land grants as impractical, but did give many of them $50 in cash.

Smith agreed and paid for Brown's move to Elba, New York, where he received 244 acres of land—sold at $1 per acre—from Smith. The deed to the land was transferred from Smith to Brown in 1849. While some of the land could not be used for farming, many of the earlier surrounding settlements remained.

When Brown staged his Kansas raid, Smith supported his military activities. When Brown raided the federal arsenal at Harper's Ferry, he carried a check for $100 in his pocket, signed by Gerrit Smith. Some believe the incident at Harper's Ferry helped fuel the Civil War. Smith believed it represented 25-years of planning to bring about a final end to slavery.[11]

Smith also befriended Frederick Douglass when he lent financial support to the publication of *Frederick Douglass' Paper* and remained in a supportive friendship with him for many years. He helped to temper Douglass away from the "moral suasion" approach of the Garrisonians, so named for William Lloyd Garrison.

The term "moral suasion" was used in a spiritual way, calling for the immediate end to slavery. Garrisonian abolitionists felt that thinking, feeling people could be persuaded by argument that slavery was wrong for moral and religious reasons, and therefore, against the ideals which founded the nation. Smith also convinced Douglass that the United States Constitution was a "pro-liberty" document and not one of "pro-slavery", as the Garrisonians claimed.

Margaret Washington, Associate Professor of History at Cornell University, adds:

"What the abolitionists didn't realize was how deeply embedded in the social, economic, and political structure slavery was. They didn't realize how powerful the "slaveocracy" was. And, they didn't realize how much racism had embedded the fabric of American life." [12]

In the Aftermath

When questioned, Smith said he was under the impression that Brown intended to create a haven for fugitive slaves in the mountains of Virginia, providing them with arms to defend themselves in the course of their escape. He said this would inspire other slaves to do the same.

Smith and the Secret Six co-conspirators of the Harper's Ferry raid knew far in advance, that their financial and moral support would literally fuel the use of weapons and violence in the raid. Collectively and individually, they denied having any knowledge of the specifics of the plot. Some may have been ambivalent regarding the use of violence; but, Brown met with the Secret Six several times in 1858 and 1859 to discuss his strategy in the attack.

In newspaper coverage of John Brown's trial, the *New York Times* and the *New York Herald* publicly linked the names of the Secret Six with Brown. Howe, Sanborn, and Stearns fled to Canada, temporarily avoiding arrest.

"We did not know that Brown meant to begin there, in Virginia, at Harper's Ferry," Sanborn said. "We expected he would go farther west, into a region less accessible, where his movements might escape notice for weeks, except as the alleged acts of some marauding party," he said.

Parker had already been staying in Italy as the guest of Robert and Elizabeth Barrett Browning. He had been infected with tuberculosis and believed the mild Italian climate would help his recovery. Gerrit Smith had his family admit him into The New York State Lunatic Asylum at Utica.[13]

Douglass' Family Life and Later Years

To say that nothing was easy in the life of Frederick Douglass is, of course, a gross misstatement; but, his personal and family life often became as turbulent as his survival and his achievements.

On one of his European speaking tours Douglass met and befriended a woman in England named Julia Griffiths. At his invitation, she came to the United States and moved into his Rochester home with his family.

Griffiths was an ambitious abolitionist, and helped to organize the finances of the *North Star* so that Douglass could eventually regain possession of his previously mortgaged home. She also tutored Douglass' children and his wife, Anna. Sadly, Anna Douglass did not respond well to the effort and remained virtually illiterate her entire life.

Scandalous rumors swept through the streets of Rochester when Douglass made Griffiths his office and business manager. As such, she scheduled his lectures, continued to keep track of the newspaper's finances, and accompanied him to every meeting. Eventually, neighbors got used to seeing the two walking arm in arm, and assumed their relationship had become something more than professional.

Griffiths was one of the six founders of the Rochester Ladies' Anti-Slavery and Sewing Society, which held festivals and bazaars to raise money for the anti-slavery initiative. They sponsored abolitionist speaking engagements, sold locally made items, as well as copies of the book *Autographs for Freedom*, which contained essays on anti-slavery by respected African American writers. By the late 1850s, the society had raised over $1,500.

They used the money to keep *Frederick Douglass' Paper* in print, to support schools for freed slaves in Kansas and Kentucky, and provide small cash gifts to fugitive slaves in the Underground Railroad network. By 1856, 136 slaves had successfully passed through Rochester on their way to Canada.

In 1855, Griffiths moved out of the Douglass home and returned to England to quiet further embarrassment for Douglass. She married soon afterwards.

~

In the same year, a German/Jewish journalist named Ottilie Assing traveled to the United States to interview Douglass and subsequently spent 22 summers with the Douglass family in Rochester. She was a passionate, politically informed abolitionist.

Their affair was not secretive and Assing believed that when Anna died, Douglass would marry her. During their separations, they wrote each other faithfully. Two years after Anna's death in 1882, Douglass did marry; however, his secretary, Helen Pitts—a white woman 20 years younger than he—became his new wife. Her family stopped speaking to her and Douglass' children felt the marriage disrespected their mother.

Helen was the daughter of Gideon Pitts, Jr., an abolitionist friend of Douglass and a "station master" of a stop on the Underground Railroad. She was a direct descendant of John and Priscilla Alden and cousin to Presidents John and John Quincy Adams. From a political perspective, the marriage of a "Mayflower daughter" to a former slave ignited criticism. To this Douglass responded," My first wife was the color of my mother; my second is the color of my father." When Ottilie Assing learned of Douglass' marriage, she went to a city park, opened a tiny vial, and swallowed its contents, potassium cyanide. She had named Douglass as the sole heir in her will.[14]

Life-points: "The Lion of Black America"

Douglass visited President Lincoln in 1863 to protest discrimination against black troops. There he received a commission in the Union Army to Recruit Negro soldiers in the South. In 1864, he served as an adviser to the president and fought for the adoption of amendments to the United States Constitution guaranteeing voting and civil liberties for African Americans.

Douglas spoke at a meeting of Negroes of New York City after officials stopped African Americans from participating in Lincoln's funeral procession through the city. Mrs. Lincoln sent Douglass the President's walking stick.

In 1870, Douglass became owner and editor of the *New National Era*, a weekly newspaper in Washington, DC. Douglass and his family moved to Washington in 1872 after his Rochester home burned to the ground. Authorities suspected arson.

In 1874, he became the first president of the Freedman's Savings and Trust Company. In 1877, Douglass was appointed a United States Marshal of the District of Columbia and he purchased "Cedar Hill", a 9-acre estate in the Anacostia section of Washington, D.C.

In 1881, Douglass was appointed Recorder of Deeds for the District of Columbia. He then published his 3rd autobiography, the *Life and Times of Frederick Douglass*.

Frederick and Helen Pitts Douglass traveled to England, France, Italy, Egypt, and Greece through 1886 and 1887. In 1888, Douglass was appointed Counsel General to Haiti by President Benjamin Harrison and in 1889, Charge d'Affaires to Santo Domingo and Resident Minister to Haiti.

In 1892, Douglass attended a historic ceremony at Kodak Park in Rochester, New York, with President Harrison, Mayor Hiram Edgerton, and Civil War Veterans.

~

Without Struggle There's No Progress

On February 20, 1895, the most powerful leader against racial injustice and supporter of human rights for all, died at home at the age of 77 after attending a women's rights meeting.[15]

Crowds gathered to pay respects at the Washington, D.C., church where Douglass' body laid in state. Parents took their children to see the famed leader for the last time. Black public schools closed. His wife and children accompanied his body back to Rochester where he was laid to rest in Mount Hope Cemetery.

At the request of Helen Pitts Douglass, Congress chartered the Frederick Douglass Memorial and Historical Association, to whom Mrs. Douglass bequeathed their home. In conjunction with the National Association of Colored Women's Clubs and the association, the house opened for visitors in 1916. In 1962, it was added to the National Park system and designated as a National Historic site in 1988.

Frederick Douglass authored 3 autobiographies: *Narrative of the Life of Frederick Douglass*, an *American Slave* (1845); *My Bondage and My Freedom* (1855), and the *Life and Times of Frederick Douglass* (1881).

Harriet Tubman (1822-1913): Woman Warrior

"I was the conductor of the Underground Railroad for eight years, and I can say what most conductors can't say; I never ran my train off the track and I never lost a passenger."

~ Harriet Tubman

Harriet Tubman, born into slavery in Dorchester County, Maryland, to parents of pure African ancestry, was literally a one-woman militia. She spent her entire life caring for, rescuing, and guiding slaves to freedom, often at her own peril. She carried a revolver for protection. According to one story, she threatened to shoot a fugitive slave in her rescue party who claimed he wanted to go back to his plantation. She pointed the gun at his head and said, "You go on or die." He made the sensible decision to continue with her into the United Province of Canada.

After she escaped to Philadelphia in 1849, she returned to Maryland to rescue her family members, traveling with them to northern locations. When congress passed the Fugitive Slave Act in 1850, her rescue efforts extended

Harriet Tubman shown here sitting far right in a rare photograph is seen with six escaped slaves she is helping to flee to Canada.

into Southern Ontario, Canada, known then as the United Province of Canada. The area still belonged to the British Empire, which had abolished slavery.

She helped freed slaves find work in their final destinations and nursed them to health when they took ill, escaping under the cover of night and guarded secrecy. She earned the name "Moses"; a nickname given her by William Lloyd Garrison, referring to the book of Exodus in which Moses led the Hebrews to freedom.

In 1851, she headed north with a group of 11 fugitive slaves and most probably stayed at the Rochester home of Frederick Douglass. "On one occasion I had eleven fugitives at the same time under my roof, and it was necessary for them to remain with me until I could collect sufficient money to get them on to Canada", he wrote in his 3rd autobiography. [16]

The Raid at Combahee Ferry

During the Civil War, Tubman worked first as an armed scout, then as a spy for the Union Army. She became the first woman to lead an armed expedition, guiding the raid at Combahee Ferry, South Carolina, where she liberated more than 700 slaves. In the summer of 1863, Tubman guided 3 steamboats around Confederate water mines leading to shore. The Union troops destroyed plantations and supplies and when they gave the signal—a series of loud whistles—slaves stampeded toward the boats and hastily boarded them.

In 1858, Tubman met John Brown. She did not advocate violence, but agreed with his Harper's Ferry plan. "General Tubman," as Brown called her, provided valuable knowledge of support stations and resources in the border states of Pennsylvania, Maryland, and Delaware. She also complied when Brown asked her to gather former slaves living in Canada for his fighting unit.

Republican United States Senator and abolitionist, William H. Seward, sold Tubman a small homestead in Auburn, New York, in 1859. The area was extremely active in anti-slavery efforts. Tubman moved her parents from Canada to Auburn where the climate was less harsh. Her home became a known haven for family, friends, boarders, and a safe place for African Americans seeking a better life.[17]

She died of pneumonia in 1913 at the Harriet Tubman Home for the Aged, a nursing home named in her honor. Surrounded by family and friends, she said, "I go to prepare a place for you", just before she died.

Harriet Beecher Stowe (1811–1896)

"So you are the little woman who wrote the book that started this Great War."
~ President Abraham Lincoln to Harriet Beecher Stowe, 1862

In Boston alone, more than 300 baby girls were named "Eva" in the year *Uncle Tom's Cabin* was published in book form. That first printing occurred on March 20, 1852, with an initial print run of 5,000 copies. In less than 1 year, the book had sold an unprecedented 300,000 copies.

Frail little Eva had captured the hearts of readers, displaying a degree of compassion and gratitude in an innocent, child-like way for the downtrodden slave, Tom. She offered him the simple Christian values of love and hope, as her author's voice eloquently cried out against slavery.[18]

The beloved book by American abolitionist and author, Harriet Beecher Stowe, galvanized the nation with its emotional portrayal of the effects of

Harriet Beecher Stowe, American abolitionist and author of *Uncle Tom's Cabin* as well as 30 other books, and travel memoirs.

slavery. Through poignant characters and fictionalized plots based on hard realities, Stowe wanted to show that no part of society could be exempt from the direct or indirect consequences of slavery. It touched everyone—masters, traders, slaves, and families, both black and white.

At the very least, Stowe's desired to educate northerners of the real horrors of slavery in the south and to urge southerners to empathize with the men, women and children who had been forced into lives of slavery.

The biggest achievement of the book, according to Stowe, is that it bravely exposed the real-life nature of slavery and attracted throngs of potential supporters as well.

Uncle Tom's Cabin represented Stowe's indignant reaction to the Fugitive Slave Law of 1850, which prohibited assistance or shelter to fugitive slaves, even in Free states. Like other anti-slavery thinkers, Stowe believed that the Fugitive Slave Act also took away the freedom of whites to do as their moral compasses dictated. She decided to shine a harsh light on the American legal system that embraced slavery and gave license to owners to mistreat slaves and avoid punishment. In some cases, the law even prevented empathetic owners from freeing their slaves, even if they chose to do so.

When she married her husband, Calvin Ellis Stowe—also an ardent abolitionist—in 1836, they moved to Brunswick, Maine, where he taught at Bowdoin College. They became actively involved with the Underground Railroad, housing fugitive slaves in their home as they crept closer to freedom in Canada.

Harriet Beecher Stowe died at 85 in Hartford, Connecticut in July of 1896, from what may have been Alzheimer's disease.[19]

Building Equality

Harriet Beecher Stowe's groundbreaking book, *Uncle Tom's Cabin*, turned attention to the social commonality between African American slaves and American women as severely disenfranchised groups, causing people to evaluate the American promise of liberty and equality for all. Stowe, single-handedly, got people thinking! The history-making Seneca Falls Women's Convention, got people doing!

The leaders and supporters of the women's movement presented a new kind of radical initiative at that convention which specifically focused on the natural rights of women, advocating for expanded education, employment, and political rights—mainly, the right to vote. At that moment in time, women learned how to write persuasively, vigorously fund-raise, and address large groups of all kinds of people with impassioned arguments.[20] In the process of fighting slavery; women found their voice and changed America.

Chapter 8
Ain't I a Woman?

"The prejudice against color, of which we hear so much,
is no stronger than that against sex. It is produced by the same cause,
and manifested very much in the same way."
~ Elizabeth Cady Stanton

The American abolitionist movement not only paved the way for but also shared the development of the long overdue women's movement, mostly because supporters of both causes understood the concept of inequality inherent in the treatment of both groups. Women had learned in their anti-slavery work how to create support networks, how to organize, and how to make social and political statements.

Assistance for both causes vividly overlapped. The individual and collective treatment of both women and African American slaves, as disenfranchised entities and likewise, deprived them of basic civil and human rights.

One of the most surprising defenders of the women's movement, particularly in western New York, was Charles Grandison Finney, known as the leading evangelist of the mid-19th century. In 1830 and 1831, he was at the peak of his career, traveling along the Erie Canal and conducting the majority of his revival meetings in Rochester's Burned Over District, where he championed the growing temperance movement. People from all walks of life flocked to his meetings. Finney preached extemporaneously and in spectacular dramatic fashion, often referring to the life events and behaviors of his followers to illustrate his main arguments. He believed that individuals could consciously will their souls to be saved.

Finney refused to be ignored. An imposing figure at 6-feet 3-inches tall, with piercing dark eyes he spoke with commanding, tremulous delivery. He

Ain't I a Woman?

gave his audiences little leeway in coming to the conclusions he envisioned for them.

Finney relied on logic, the power of persuasion and playing on the emotions of hope and fear to convert his listeners. He rejected the traditional view that the Gospel held complex and confusing theologies by presenting it in simpler ways. This was a pioneering approach, sometimes referred to as "scientific method" or "new measures" in revivalism at the time. This method would be successfully adapted as a model by future revivalists, right up to the present day. One of his followers stated on recorded that, "Brother Finney doesn't preach; he just explains what all the other fellows are preaching about."[1]

The "Cult of Domesticity"

While Finney did not singularize women's place in his revival meetings as such, he did not limit his soul saving to men only. Finney preached salvation through individual reform. This would manifest in social reform and in the growing movements of the day, including temperance, anti-slavery, and the fight for women's rights.

In pursuing salvation for all souls, Finney expanded the role of women at revival meetings for the first time, where he encouraged them to pray or speak out loud in the presence of both men and women. Critics deemed the practice "promiscuous" behavior in public assemblies. They considered it "dangerous" as it publicly implied equality between the sexes. For women, it was a profound step in the right direction.[2]

The phrase "cult of domesticity" was often used to describe 19th century attitudes and expectations toward women. To speak or pray out loud violated the belief that married women should restrict their activities to home and family. It was also viewed as a wife's rejection of her husband's marital authority, which portrayed men as superior and women, as unimportant subordinate partners with limited intellectual abilities. These exact descriptions had also been attributed to African American slaves.

In Finney's view, his egalitarian approach to women's spirituality or "biblical feminism" promoted women's rights in religious expression. His meetings would also provide for the sharing of testimony and preaching by women, which furthered the goals of the women's movement. Lay-witnessing by women, including home visits by contingents of women and their special prayer meeting groups, became usual occurrences and served as the impetus to engage larger community participation.

The degree to which Finney enlisted the help of his second wife Elizabeth Ford Atkins, a Rochester widow, in his religious and social campaigns, reflected his impact on the women's movement. Elizabeth became one of the first women to speak at revival meetings; she prayed aloud and formed prayer groups and home visits with other wives.

The Finneys traveled to England twice during the 1850s, where Charles preached in the same ways he addressed his followers in America. As she had done at home, Elizabeth began holding meetings for women, starting a trend that would become an accepted practice. Twenty years after his fiery beginnings in Rochester, Finney had built a religious bridge across the Atlantic.

Oberlin, Ohio: Educating African Americans and Women

In 1832, Finney became minister of the Chatham Street Chapel in New York City. With the help of anti-slavery supporter, Lewis Tappan, he founded the Broadway Tabernacle, a Congregationalist church on West 93rd Street.

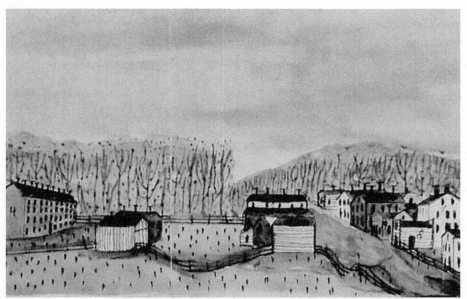

Charles G. Finney was appointed professor of theology at Oberlin College shown here in rare 1835 sketch. Finney would go on to become president of the college in 1852.

Ain't I a Woman?

Soon, Finney wanted to teach his evangelical principles in a facility established primarily for that purpose. The Tappan brothers provided the financial means to help Finney, as a professor, found a college in Oberlin, Ohio, in approximately 1835. Here, he would offer an evangelical education in a socially reformed setting which would become Oberlin College, the first of its kind to welcome women and African Americans, among others.[3]

Oberlin was the first American college to allow African Americans and white people to eat together at the same table and to have women and African Americans study in the same classrooms as white men. Finney became the first president of Oberlin College in 1851. He served as pastor of the First Congregational Church in Oberlin from 1837-1872, as he maintained his revivalist services in the northeast, as well.

Oberlin, Ohio, was also recognized as a prominent stop on the Underground Railroad. Families and anti-slavery supporters there hid and moved fugitive slaves along in their passage north and into Canada.

Seneca County: The Birth of the Women's Rights Movement

Hastily organized and minimally advertised as "a convention to discuss the social, civil, and religious condition and rights of women", The Seneca Falls Convention of 1848 ignited the women's movement of the mid-19th century and beyond.

The first gathering of its kind in the United States, the convention spanned two days—July 19 and July 20—at the Wesleyan Chapel in Seneca Falls, New York. The importance of the event and the attention it attracted would result in subsequent women's rights conventions. Only 2 weeks later another convened in Rochester and, in 1850, one in Worcester, Massachusetts, the first in a series of annual meetings.[4]

Abolitionists Elizabeth Cady and Lucretia Mott organized the Seneca Falls Convention. The two met in 1840 at the World Anti-Slavery Convention in London, England. As women, they were barred from entering the convention floor and from participating in the issues of anti-slavery on a global level.

Their mutual indignation at this rebuff—the kind of treatment women everywhere experienced—steered them to a more positive, yet pro-active decision. They would organize a convention of their own, for and by women.[5]

Stanton lived near Seneca Falls and due to its strategic proximity to

Cayuga Lake and the Erie Canal, used her home as convention headquarters as she and Mott prepared for their meeting. The activities of the first day, Wednesday, July 19, were to be "exclusively for women". On the second day, "other ladies and gentlemen" had been scheduled to address the convention.

The agenda of the convention included demands for women's equality in education, work, law, politics, religion, family life, and moral or marital authority. It also addressed the methods women's groups would use to spread their messages, including hiring lecturers, circulating written tracts and essays, signing petitions, enlisting help from churches and newspapers, and continuing to hold conventions.

Declaration of Sentiments and Grievances

On the first day of the convention, before 300 attendees, Stanton read the document she and Mott had written called the *Declaration of Sentiments and Grievances*. Modeled on the Declaration of Independence it began with a preamble that similarly announced, "We hold these truths to be self-evident: that all men and women are created equal; that they are endowed by their Creator with certain inalienable rights...".[6]

The document immediately captured the nation's attention, as it succinctly linked women's rights with the founding ideals of the United States government. Their Declaration detailed the injustices forced upon women in the United States and challenged them to organize and draw up petitions for specific rights. Frederick Douglass addressed the convention on the second day, when the assembly present adopted and signed the Declaration. The convention passed 12 resolutions. The 9th resolution, however, was the only one that brought opposition, stating, "It is the duty of the women of this country to secure to themselves their sacred right to the elective franchise" or their right to vote. A lengthy debate between Stanton and Douglass followed, in which he supported the importance of "female enfranchisement", and the resolution passed.[7]

This particular outcome of the Seneca Falls Convention was met with a degree of public ridicule, prompting some to remove their support. Yet, the deed had been done. The passage of the resolution for women's right to vote marked the beginning of the women's suffrage movement in America.[8]

Ain't I a Woman?

The Women
Elizabeth Cady Stanton (1815-1902)

"Oh, my daughter, I wish you were a boy."

A young Elizabeth Cady was shocked when she tried to console her father after the death of her brother, Eleazar. She assured him that she would fill her brother's place, to which Daniel Cady replied, "Oh, my daughter, I wish you were a boy." Stanton would record that moment in her memoirs, which imprinted the message that boys held more value than girls.

Daniel Cady worked as a Federalist attorney, a circuit court judge, and a New York Supreme Court Justice. Elizabeth would peruse his law library and discuss cases with his law clerks. She soon observed that the law disproportionately favored men over women, leaving them without legal rights to property, income, employment, or even actual custody of their children. In fact, their roles resembled those of slaves.

Elizabeth Cady Stanton was a leading figure in the early women's rights movement. Stanton addressed various issues including the right to vote, parental custody rights, property rights, and birth control.

Stanton viewed these inequalities as egregious slights to women and vowed to correct them.

Elizabeth met Henry Brewster Stanton though her cousin, Gerrit Smith. Stanton was an anti-slavery orator and attorney. At their wedding ceremony in 1840, Elizabeth requested that the minister remove the phrase "promise to obey" from the wedding vows. While she enjoyed motherhood, Elizabeth lacked intellectual challenge and became involved in women's rights issues. During this time, she met Rochester resident, Susan B. Anthony.

Stanton is the author of her autobiography, the *Woman's Bible*, *Eighty*

Years & More: Reminiscences 1815-1897, and the *Solitude of Self, or Self-Sovereignty*, which she first delivered as a speech at the 1892 convention of the National American Woman's Suffrage Association in Washington, D.C. She served as president of the Association from 1892 until 1900.

She died of heart failure at her home in New York City on October 26, 1902, 18 years before congress granted women the right to vote in the United States. She was buried in Woodlawn Cemetery in the Bronx. The Elizabeth Cady Stanton House in Seneca Falls is part of the Women's Rights National Historical Park.[9]

Susan B. Anthony (1820-1906)

"Men, their rights, and nothing more;
women, their rights, and nothing less."

Susan Brownell Anthony was born in Adams, Massachusetts, and raised in the Quaker faith, which believed in the equality of all God's creatures. The fact that Anthony's father had been rebuked by his congregation for marrying a non-Quaker and subsequently disowned from his church for allowing a dance school to operate in his home, served to strengthen his propensity for equal and just social reform.[10]

He encouraged all his children, boys and girls alike, to learn how to be self-supporting, teaching them business principles and giving them family responsibilities at an early age. When they moved to Rochester not coincidentally, via the Erie Canal in 1845, the Anthony farmstead soon became the Sunday afternoon

Susan B. Anthony was an American feminist who played a pivotal role in the Women's Suffrage Movement. She was harshly ridiculed at the time, accused of trying to destroy the institution of marriage.

gathering place for local reform activists, including Susan's lifelong friend, Frederick Douglass.

The Civil War had slowed the progress of the women's rights movement; but, in 1866 Anthony and Elizabeth Cady Stanton organized the American Equal Rights Association (AERA). Their organization supported the right of universal suffrage for all, without restriction of race, sex, belief, wealth, or social status. Anthony had found her niche and for the rest of her life, lived almost entirely on fees earned as a speaker. With Stanton, Anthony also began publishing a weekly newspaper devoted to women's rights, called the *Revolution*.

According to historian, Ann D. Gordon, "By the end of the Civil War, Susan B. Anthony occupied new social and political territory. She was emerging on the national scene as a female leader, something new in American history, and she did so as a single woman in a culture that perceived the spinster as anomalous and unguarded. By the 1880s, she was among the senior political figures in the United States." [11]

United States v. Susan B. Anthony

Despite the fact that nearly 50 women in Rochester attempted to vote in the 1872 presidential election, with 15 of them actually casting ballots, Anthony's attempt was thwarted by her arrest for voting illegally.

In 1893, she began the Rochester branch of the Women's Educational and Industrial Union and the Rochester Council of Women in 1898. She also raised the necessary funds to admit women to the University of Rochester.

Anthony did not live to see the achievement of women's suffrage at the national level. At the time of her death, women had achieved suffrage in Wyoming, Utah, Colorado, and Idaho, with several larger states following suit, and legal rights for married women had been established in most states.

The Nineteenth Amendment, giving women the right to vote, was popularly known as the Susan B. Anthony Amendment. After it's ratification in 1920, the National American Woman Suffrage Association, whose policies had been strongly influenced by Anthony, transformed into the League of Women Voters.

Susan B. Anthony died of heart failure and pneumonia at the age of 86 in her Rochester home on March 13, 1906. She was buried at Mount Hope Cemetery in Rochester. [12]

Lucretia Mott (1793-1880)

"Women's right to the elective franchise should be yielded to her, whether she exercises that right or not." [3]

Lucretia Coffin Mott—American Quaker, abolitionist, and women's rights activist—was born in Nantucket, Massachusetts. Like Elizabeth Cady Stanton, as a young woman Mott experienced that males were treated differently and regarded more highly than women. After graduating from the Nine Partners School, run by the Society of Friends in Dutchess County, New York, she became employed as a teacher there. Almost immediately, she developed an interest in women's rights when she learned that male teachers earned three times the salary of female teachers.

When her family moved to Philadelphia, she went with them, along with fellow teacher, James Mott. Lucretia and James married in 1811. She became a Quaker minister in 1821 and,

Lucretia Mott was a Quaker, abolitionist, women's rights activist and social reformer. She helped write the *Declaration of Sentiment* during the Seneca Falls Convention of 1848.

with her husband's support, traveled widely preaching the benefits of the Quaker's "inward light" and the presence of the Divine Spirit in every person.

In 1833, James Mott helped found the American Anti-Slavery Society. Lucretia was the only woman to speak at the Society's first organizational meeting. At the urging of both black and white female attendees, Mott founded the Philadelphia Female Anti-Slavery Society. This decision was in response to the male-dominated policies of the American Anti-Slavery Society and other abolitionist groups. These associations denied membership to women and they were not to "sit, speak, vote, hold office or otherwise have the rights of persons of the other sex."

Women's participation in the anti-slavery movement threatened the social structure of the time and many men in the abolitionist movement frowned upon public assemblage and speeches by women. When Mott met Elizabeth Cady Stanton at the World Anti-Slavery Convention in London in 1840, their plans would forever change the destiny of the women's movement. While Stanton is historically credited as the leader of the women's suffrage movement, Mott's mentoring of their work together propelled the movement forward.

In 1849, Mott's *Sermon to the Medical Students* was published and, in 1850, her speech, *Discourse on Woman*, followed. In 1864, Mott and other Hicksite Quakers incorporated Swarthmore College in Pennsylvania—one of the earliest co-educational colleges in the United States—which remains a premier liberal-arts college in the country today. By 1906, Swarthmore had become officially non-sectarian.

Lucretia Mott died of pneumonia in 1880 at her home in Cheltenham, Pennsylvania, and was buried in the Quaker Fairhill Burial Ground in North Philadelphia.[13]

Amy and Isaac Post: Radical Quakerism

In her day, Rochester resident, Amy Post (1802-1889), became a well-known abolitionist, feminist, freethinker and radical Quaker. A staunch supporter of women's rights, Post, of course, did not know or intend that she and her neighbors, Elizabeth Cady Stanton and Susan B. Anthony, would become famous in the women's movement and, in turn, promote Rochester as a hub of similar activity.

Amy Post, along with her husband Isaac, became members of the radical Hicksite movement when the traditional Quaker Church came out against their involvement in the struggle for abolitionism and women's rights.

Amy Post was one of many women of her day who attempted to lead good, ethical lives and to improve the lives of those around them. Her Quaker upbringing honed her attention on social problems, their causes, and ways to deal with them. Quaker principles offered networks of social support to those in need, practiced the equality of men and women, relied on extended circles of kinship, maintained faith in one's inner light, and demonstrated a commitment to humanitarian reforms.[14]

Quaker tenets compelled women to speak and preach out loud in their meetings. They considered it to be true adherence to their religion. Everyone had a responsibility to preach, not just clergy or scholars. The written word was relatively unimportant compared with testimony from one's inner light.

For many, the simple benefits of being a Quaker—guidance by inward inspiration and seeing the Divine in everyone—grew to include a wider or more radical definition of seeing or hearing from the Divine via their participation and belief in spiritualism—a rampant phenomenon in 1848. Amy and her husband, Isaac, were among the early converts to the spiritualism movement.

The fascinating concept that believers received legitimate messages from the spirits of deceased men and women telling them to exert greater efforts in their reform movements, gained growing support. For women, who made up the majority of known spiritualists, messages from the other side were perceived as special communications to them which negated the power of men in the realm of religion. Thus, many prominent female spiritualists readily supported the abolition of slavery and the achievement of women's suffrage.

Despite the proliferation of feminine spiritualism, Amy's husband, Isaac (1798-1872), managed to become a recognized medium. In 1852, his book, *Voices from the Spirit World, Being Communications from Many Spirits*, was published. It claims to include spirit writings from Benjamin Franklin and George Fox (one of the founders of Quakerism or the Religious Society of Friends).

During this period, Amy maintained her attachment to the free thought movement, radical Quakerism and spiritualism. All three schools of thought grew from opposition to traditional Christianity. And, all three drew participants in the abolition and women's rights movements.

Under the powerful guidance of Elias Hicks of Jericho, New York, the "Hicksite Quakers" led a strong initiative against the predominant Quaker Friends, arguing that they had wandered too far from their simple religious roots.

Ain't I a Woman?

The fiery preacher urged a return to the tried-and-true principles of their religion: reliance on one's inner light for messages from the Divine. Ultimately, the Quaker group divided into the Orthodox Friends and the Hicksite Friends.

In 1848, Amy attended the Rochester Women's Rights Convention, as her first venture into the women's movement. Through 1849 and 1850, she and her sister organized anti-slavery fairs in western New York, signing their public statements with just their first and last names, omitting a "Miss" or "Mrs." in their signatures. Amy and Isaac also provided shelter for fugitive slaves, especially for women slaves fleeing from sexual abuse.[15]

The "Rochester Knockings"

In the same year, the Posts befriended and took into their Rochester home the Fox Sisters; spiritualists Kate (1837-1892) and Margaret (1833-1893) claimed to have the ability to communicate with spirits through a series of raps or knocks during their sessions or séances. The Posts introduced them to their radical-thinking circle of friends, making many of them ardent believers in spiritualism.

In an 1853 letter, friend and spiritualist, Sarah Thayer, stated to Amy Post that the lesson of spiritualism was that a woman "ought to be better qualified to direct the spiritual life of her own sex than any belov'd disciple or even Jesus himself as a man or a brother."

A surprising fact regarding the Fox Sisters was their ability to become self-supporting without the aid of or approval of male management of their careers as spiritualists. Older sister, Leah (1814-1890), even served as their booking manager.[16]

The Fox Sisters played a pivotal role in the modern spiritualism movement but were also considered by many to be societies "original feminists" due to their being able to financial support themselves conducting séances.

In 1888, the sisters confessed under duress that the premise of their séances and prevalent rapping's from those who had crossed over, were a complete hoax and publicly demonstrated how they produced the desired effects. Margaret attempted to recant her confession the following year, but the reputation of the otherworldly Fox sisters had been damaged beyond repair. The admission ruined their hefty financial gain and standing in the community.

In less than 5 years, they died in dismal poverty. Spiritualism, however, continued as if the confessions of the Fox sisters had never happened.[17]

Sojourner Truth (1797-1883)

"Where did your Christ come from? From God and a woman!
Men had nothing to do with Him."

Born as Isabella Baumfree in 1797 in Hurley, New York, Sojourner Truth was a noble figure in both the abolitionist movement and in the fight for women's rights.

In 1843 she changed her name to Sojourner Truth to embody the core of her message and personal belief that God had presented her with a holy message against slavery. "The spirit calls me and I must go", she explained to friends before she began her tireless journey, traveling, and preaching.[18]

At 6-feet-tall, possessing a proud spirit, indefatigable drive, and unwavering faith in the Lord above, Truth is best remembered for her brief, but powerful extemporaneous speech at the Ohio Women's Right Convention in 1851. She was 54-years-old at the time. The speech was subsequently titled *Ain't I a Woman?*

As she strode to the podium to speak, comments such as "not another speech by an abolitionist", wafted through the crowd. With characteristic strength, calm, and eloquence, she delivered her history making remarks for women's rights, challenging her listeners to acknowledge equality between the sexes and hushing hecklers by reminding them that God says to "Honor thy father and thy mother".

"Well, children, where there is so much racket there must be something out of kilter. I think that between the Negros's of the South and the women at the North, all talking about rights, the white men will be in a fix pretty soon. But what's all this here talking about?

Ain't I a Woman?

That man over there say that women needs to be helped into carriages, lifted over ditches, and to have the best place everywhere. Nobody ever helps me into carriages, or over mud-puddles, or gives me any best place! And ain't I a woman? Look at me! Look at my arm! I have ploughed, and planted, and gathered into barns, and no man could head me! And ain't I a woman? I could work as much and eat as much as a man-when I could get it-and bear the lash as well! And ain't I a woman? And when I cried out with my mother's grief, none but Jesus heard me. And ain't I a woman?

Then they talk about this thing in the head; what's this they call it? ['Intellect' someone whispers near.] That's right, honey. What's that got to do with women's rights or Negros's rights? If my cup won't hold but a pint, and yours holds a quart, wouldn't you be mean not to let me have my little half-measure full?

I SELL THE SHADOW TO SUPPORT THE SUBSTANCE.
SOJOURNER TRUTH.

Sojourner Truth was born into slavery with the slave name Isabella (Bella) Baumfree. She later escaped with her daughter and later sued to recover her son. She won becoming the first black women to win such a law suit against a white man. During the 1851 Ohio Women's Rights Convention she delivered her iconic speech, *Ain't I a Woman*.

Then that little man in black there, he says women can't have as much rights as men, because Christ wasn't a woman! Where did your Christ come from? From God and a woman! Men had nothing to do with Him.

If the first woman God ever made was strong enough to turn the world upside down all alone, these women together ought to be able to turn it back, and get it right side up again! And now that they are asking to do it, the men better let them! Obliged to you for hearing me, and now old Sojourner has got nothing more to say."[19]

She delivered other memorable speeches, gauging her presentations on the dynamics of each crowd, intermittently weaving Biblical references into her statements. She addressed the American Equal Rights Association in 1867, where she spoke mainly about rights for black women, reiterating, "we should keep things going while things are stirring". Throughout her life, she was thought of as the most powerful African American woman to consistently and publicly link the oppression of slavery with the subjection of women.

On New Year's Day, 1871, Truth addressed the crowd at the Eighth Anniversary of Negro Freedom. The thrust of her message referenced freed slaves who lived on government aid, paid for by taxpayers, making the point that this arrangement did not help either party. She suggested that black people be given their own land to cultivate toward self-sufficiency.

Legal Victory

Sojourner Truth was a consummate fighter and used the legal system to her advantage. In 1828, she became the first black woman to take a white man to court and win. She sued him for illegally selling her son, Peter, to a plantation owner in Alabama.

Sojourner Truth died on November 26, 1883, at her home in Battle Creek, Michigan, and was buried at Oak Hill Cemetery in Battle Creek beside other family members.[20]

~

One of the greatest contributors to the women's movement of the 19th century— faithfully working all hours of the day and night—was unquestionably the Erie Canal which supported an army of packet boats traveling the length of upstate New York. This powerful waterway carried a flotilla of radicals, visionaries, social reformers, and prophets bent on the idea of a creating a new society. It ushered historic figures along the Atlantic seaboard and through the cities and towns of western New York, carrying speakers to engagements and eventually, women to voting booths.[21]

Remembering the words of Sojourner Truth: "We should keep things going while things are stirring". America would never be the same.

Chapter 9
The Psychic Highway

Today, the Erie Canal National Heritage Corridor is a recreational place used for its own diverse array of social traffic and for the option of spending time in the great outdoors. It is an incredible engineering achievement which houses human and political history.

It is a busy thoroughfare for walkers and joggers, young and old, alike and for parents pushing their cherubs in state-of-the-art strollers. Maybe you'll meet an energized bicycle/blogger with a mission to visit each canal community, who quickly makes room for roller-blading kids whizzing by. You may even see the occasional houseboat lazily floating on the river below. Some people study nature and some study human nature, perhaps creating fictional stories or humorous biographies for the most eccentric looking subjects.[1]

It's safe to say that the last thing these folks think about is how this mammoth creation, the Erie Canal, not only changed the history of transportation in America; but how it also changed the character and spirit of 19th century Americans.

The Erie Canal delivered people to important places for important reasons, like Seneca Falls for history's first women's convention, to Rochester to meet and support people like Frederick Douglass and Susan B. Anthony, or to witness the Fox Sisters summon spirits with their eerie knockings. Maybe people on the temperance bandwagon were hurrying to the Burned Over District so Charles Grandison Finney could save their souls.

It was a time of intense individual focus and enlightened change in the ways in which people communicated. It was as if a bolt of electricity struck western New York, lighting it up as fertile ground for ideas and lifestyles that had never been expressed or attempted before. It was a time of religious re-birth, ongoing social reform and making one's life the best it could be in the present, in the future... and even in the great beyond.[2]

The "Eerie" Canal

Historian Whitney Cross, born in Rochester in 1913, dubbed the Erie Canal "the Psychic Highway", for the over-abundance of spiritual schools of thought and movements that graced its 524-mile span across a multiple-canal system in upstate New York.

His chosen title specifically recognized the proliferation of spiritualism and rampant psychic beliefs and notions centering on the paranormal, including every unexplainable bump in the night; on souls, lost and found; on ghosts and scribbled messages from the afterlife, courtesy of Benjamin Franklin and his contemporaries.

Every manner of mysticism permeated the path of the Erie Canal, the more creepy and uncanny, the better. Enough activity passed along its route to easily catapult psychic thought into the 20th and 21st centuries without a single farewell séance![3]

"A Thoroughfare of the Occult"

In his book, *Listen for a Lonesome Drum: a New York State Chronicle*, author and folklorist, Carl Carmer, calls the "hilly strip scarcely twenty-five miles wide"—from east of Albany to west of Buffalo—"a thoroughfare of the occult", referring to several locations along the route of the Erie Canal. He believes these places earned their inclusion in the category of things odd or supernatural, in a New York State kind of way.[4]

One scholarly view of why these places seem to be more conducive to the acceptance of psychic reports, has to do with an attraction to the aesthetic or romantic nature of the places themselves and the need for the residents to define them as unique in a weird or unsettling way.[5]

Of particular significance to Carmer in this compact 25-mile sweep are spiritually noteworthy locations. Some of these are the Niskayuna Shaker

The Psychic Highway

Family Dwellings in Albany, including the Ann Lee Home, so named for the founder of the Shaker religion, a Sufi community called the Abode of the Message, and the Sulak Academy, in what used to be the Mount Lebanon South Family Shaker Village, about 24 miles southeast of Albany. The community teaches meditation, concentration, prayer, and the Sufi concepts of breath, sacred sound, and light.

In Oneida, the Oneida Community—a religious social group most active from approximately 1848 to 1880—was one of the most radical in its belief in a Utopian Society. The 93,000-square-foot Mansion House, where the original group of "Perfectionists" lived and worked together, still exists as a National Historic Landmark.[6]

Cobbs Hill in Rochester, now a park, was the intended site, in 1843, of the Second Coming, according to William Miller (founder of the Millerites). The town of Penn Yan (a shortened version of "Pennsylvania Yankee") in the Finger Lakes Region was the home of Jemima Wilkinson, known as the Public Universal Friend and founder of the Jemimakins. Many believed Wilkinson died of the plague, and then returned to life to found a Quaker colony on the shores of Seneca Lake, based on total sexual abstinence and the Ten Commandments.[7]

Hydesville, New York, is the site of the original home of the Fox Sisters, known as the creators of Modern Spiritualism. The house still exists and devotees continue to make pilgrimages there. Mormons from all over the world faithfully visit Hill Cumorah in Palmyra, where in 1827, Mormon founder Joseph Smith received the "golden plates" that contained the principles of the faith that would later become the Book of Mormon.

Lily Dale or the Lily Dale Assembly in Lily Dale, New York, essentially embraces its original purpose created in 1879: to provide a camp and meeting place for spiritualists and freethinkers. It is the world's largest center for the "science, philosophy, and religion of spiritualism". The facility offers astrological readings, sweat lodges, spirit walks, and sessions with mediums. Here, guests flock to the Inspiration Stump to feel the profound energy of the place and receive messages from spirits. Located south of Buffalo, Lily Dale regularly attracts people from all across the United States and Canada.[8]

THE PSYCHIC HIGHWAY

Guardian Spirits and Native Energies

Joscelyn Godwin, English-born author and Professor of Music at Colgate University, explains how religious and spiritual movements in upstate New York were brought to the area by "spiritual outsiders", leaving palpable energies in the areas they frequented. In his book, *Upstate Cauldron*, Godwin reveals an additional 40 or more relatively unfamiliar spiritual groups and leaders who impacted upstate New York society from 1776 through 1914 and also includes a current listing of approximately 150 relevant sites to entice present-day travelers.

Godwin also addresses Native American theology—particularly among the Iroquois—who relied upon the events, images, and personalities revealed in dreams to guide or demand human choices and actions in life. One important example of this is found in the initiation of young native males, who were required to spend 2 weeks alone, fasting in the forest. They believed this ordeal, if successful, would culminate in the manifestation of their guardian spirits, who would replace their parents as protectors and counselors. The experience may also have resulted in designating some boys as clairvoyants, shamans, and witches. Many Americans placed faith in Native American spirit guides.[9]

Mason Winfield is the prolific author of several books, each focusing on some aspect of New York State's psychic/spiritual history and how it is experienced, today. He writes of spirits along the Niagara Wine Trail, ghosts of those who fought in the War of 1812 (also called the Niagara War), Iroquoian zombie-like incarnations of their predecessors, and apparitions of Benedict Arnold in Saratoga, the "Spa City", and more. He speaks of village ghosts in western New York's old Seneca Territory and explains how even the simple flora and fauna of the place may be conduits for spirits, as well.

His first book, *Shadows of the Western Door*, deals with how white settlers in western New York—more than any other group new to North America— became mystified by the strong spiritual aura of the Iroquois Confederacy (the Mohawk, Oneida, Onondaga, Cayuga, Seneca, and Tuscarora tribes), with its 1,000-year-history. The Iroquois were, perhaps, some of the most creative and inspiring storytellers on earth and held sway in the dissemination of supernatural information from the Hudson and Mohawk River Valleys, westward to the Finger Lakes region to Niagara Falls and beyond.

Also known as the Haundenosaunee or the People of the Long House, the Iroquois lived and believed in a multi-level existence, with supernatural entities, places, and traditions existing in and around all stages of life. Indeed, the ground visitors walk upon today may hold potent spiritual energy buried there a long time ago.

Winfield's references are replete with such things as shape shifting witches, ethereal lights, vampires, and zombie-like manifestations. He describes the "telepathic stalkers" who know and control our thoughts and actions, odd or abnormal looking animals, cursed land, and haunted hills. His tales include miraculous healings by Tuscarora medicine men Mad Bear (1927-1985) and Ted Williams (1930-2005), which were practiced in traditional and spiritual wisdom, spiritual knowledge, and in their search for higher consciousness among the Six Nations of the Iroquois Confederacy.

Winfield also offers regularly scheduled Ghost Walks in and around sites in western New York, one of which is called, "Canal side!"[10]

High-Tech Ghost Hunting in the 21st Century

It's human nature for people to want answers for the things we can't explain. Even after the Fox Sisters came clean about how they manifested their well-timed rapping's and summoned spirits of the dead to their séance table, people believed then, and still do, that there are unaccountable energies and psychic vestiges around us now, of people, places and things that have long passed. Isn't it also human to want to communicate with and bring them back to us, in some shape or form?

Central New York Paranormal Research is at your service—and never charges a fee—to investigate disturbing or troublesome claims of unusual, unexplainable paranormal activity in homes and businesses all across New York State.[11]

These professionals are serious about responding to clients' requests, with the caveat that the business of dealing with paranormal activity is best left to people who know how to conduct the proceedings. Not all spirits are friendly and the unfriendly ones may be capable of wreaking emotional and psychological havoc upon unsuspecting and/or ill-equipped victims.

Founded in 2004 by Michael Ciulla and Marc Vitrella, with current lead investigator, Kevin Gardner, and Adam Squadrito, Tech Manager, CNYPR plays down the stereotypical image of reality TV ghost hunting. Its investigations are generated by home and business client referrals, including those from churches and religious parishes across the state. All communication and any "evidence" gathered is not disclosed to the public but kept in strict confidentiality with clients, only.

The team includes retired law enforcement officers, fire fighters, paramedics, nurses, and those with backgrounds in public service. The CNYPR staff has education and experience in the fields of criminal justice, human behavior, psychology, TV production, and editing.

They specifically advise potential clients to refrain from attempting to conduct their own investigations and/or from using Ouija boards. The danger in not following their instructions could possibly intensify the problem, if one already exists.

The Ouija board has traditionally been a popular way to contact "the other side", usually as a lighthearted party novelty. However, the team is adamant that it not be used prior to one of their investigations, because they believe sometimes the board does work, and its "contacts", can bring uninvited spirits of the vilest kind into the human realm. These contacts, according to CNYPR, are those residing in the lowest levels of the astral planes they occupy (where there are lower vibrations of ether), allowing them to more easily emerge. Their intentions are most often destructive and dangerous.

If a home or business is suspected of being haunted and its residents opt for a paranormal investigation, clients are asked many questions first. The team needs to know if anyone in the residence is ill, is having nightmares, if hot or cold spots are detected, or if pets' behaviors changed unexpectedly. They take notes if unexplained knocks, bangs, footsteps or other sounds have been heard; if clients hear voices or laughing; if they feel they have been touched, scratched or pushed by some invisible force; if shadows or apparitions (fuzzy, ghostlike images) have been seen, but cannot be traced or explained; and other pertinent details.

For those who prefer a more hands-on, social networking type of experience in ghost hunting or ghost busting, there is Shadowlands Ghosts and Haunting website. It contains true stories and interviews by site owners, Mike Juliano and Tina Carlson, help and advice, a listing of haunted places and galleries of photos, videos, and EVPs (Electronic Voice Phenomena).[12]

The Psychic Highway

Mother Knows Best

You don't call. You don't write. But, you do commune with Mother Nature. Now, what Mom wouldn't appreciate that?

Madis Senner, former global money manager turned spiritualist and author, found that there is nothing more healing—physically, spiritually, emotionally and psychically—than time spent with Mother Earth. This belief most closely resembles the powerful principles of Native American mysticism.

"She" lives in upstate New York, more exactly in the vicinity of the Erie Canal, says Senner, nestling her abilities in what he calls "fields of consciousness". Immersing oneself in prayer or meditation at one of Mother Earth's fields can positively and powerfully transform you. Any kind of prayer will do, believes Senner, including meditation, contemplation, mantra, praise, petition, thanks, visualization, and others.

In 2002, he first felt called to encourage groups of people to pray in and around the area of Onondaga Lake, considered to be a sacred Native American site in Syracuse, New York. It is called the Peacemaker Sanctuary. Today, he leads workshops in spiritual consciousness, the power of thought, and meditations to bring people closer to Mother Earth in and around the communities along the Erie Canal. Locations of sacred sites are listed here: http://www.jubileeinitiative.org/sacredsites.html

Many of these sites are off the beaten path. So, too, were the countless variations of psychic belief and expression so prevalent in 19th century New York—and remarkable enough to exist and thrive, today.[13]

~

Were people like Henry Hudson, Charles Finney, Frederick Douglass, Sojourner Truth, and of course, Jesse Hawley and DeWitt Clinton, psychic? Were they visionaries? Were they dreamers?

Indeed these people of great mental and spiritual acuity conceived ideas just as astounding as any paranormal communication with anyone or anything not readily of-this-world. In fact, spiritualists seemed to have a much easier time contacting spirits than the forefathers of the Erie Canal did in selling the project to mortal men and bringing it to fruition and its final glorious completion!

The Psychic Highway

Where there is progress, there is change, economically and socially. Because of the Erie Canal, New York State didn't simply eke its way into historic transformation; it exploded into the 19th century in ways that galvanized all aspects of American life.

Bibliography

Applegate, Debby (2006) The Most Famous Man in America: The Biography of Henry Ward Beecher. Doubleday Religious Publishing Group.
Barnes, Joseph W. Historic Broad Street Bridge and the Erie Canal Sesquicentennial, 1825-1975. (In Rochester History, vol. XXXVII, no. 3, July 1975)

Bernstein, Peter L. Wedding of the waters: the Erie Canal and the making of a great nation. (W.W. Norton & Co., 2005)

Boyd, Robert & Silk, Joan. How Humans Evolved (New York: Norton, 1997).

Bradford, Sarah Hopkins (orig. pub. 1886), (1961). Harriet Tubman: The Moses of Her People> New York: Corinth Books.

Brodhead, John Romeyn. History of the State of New York. Harper & Brothers; 1874.

Brodie, Fawn M. No Man Knows My History: The Life of Joseph Smith (2nd ed.), New York: Alfred A. Knopf, 1971

Bushman, Richard Lyman. Joseph Smith: Rough Stone Rolling. Vintage Books, 2007

Douglass, Frederick. The Narrative of the Life of Frederick Douglass, an American Slave. Written by Himself.

Francis, John Wakefield. "Reminiscences of Christopher Colles". The Atlantic Souvenir. New York. 1859

Hosack, David. Memoir of DeWitt Clinton. New York: J. Seymour, 1829.

Jefferson Papers, Library of Congress
Jefferson to Clinton, Monticello, December 12, 1822. Polygraph copy available online from the Library of Congress.

Johnson Paul E. A Shopkeeper's Millennium: Society and Revivals in Rochester, New York 1815-1837, Hill and Wang 1978.

Johnson, Paul E. The Kingdom of Matthias: A Story of Sex and Salvation in 19th-Century America, Oxford University Press, 2012

Ketchum, Richard M. Divided Loyalties: How the American Revolution Came to New York. New York: Henry Holt, 2002

Klees, Emerson. The Erie Canal in the Finger Lakes region: the heart of New York State; photography by C.S. Kenyon. (Friends of the Finger Lakes Publishing, 1996)

Klees, Emerson. The Crucible of Ferment: New York's "Psychic Highway", Cameo Press, 2001

Knight, George R. (1995). Millennial Fever and the End of the World. Pacific Press.

Koeppel, Gerard. Bond of Union: building the Erie Canal and the American Empire (Da Capo Press, 2009)

McFee, Michele A. A Long haul: the story of the New York State Barge Canal. (Purple Mountain Press, 1998)

Bibliography

McKelvey, Blake. Rochester and the Erie Canal. (Rochester History, vol. XI, nos. 3-4, July 1949)

Merrill, Arch. A River Ramble: Saga of the Genesee Valley, Louis Heindle & Son, 1943.

Merrill, Arch. The Towpath, Louis Heindl & Son, 1945

Merrill, Arch. The White Women and Her Valley: Mary Jemison. American Books-Stratford Press, 1961

Merrill, Arch. Tomahawks and Old Lace: Tales of Western New York, Henderson-Mosher, 1948.

Merwick, Donna The Shame and the Sorrow: Dutch-Amerindian Encounters in New Netherland (Philadelphia: University of Pennsylvania Press, 2006);

O'Keef, Rose. Frederick and Anna Douglass in Rochester, N.Y., History Press, 2013

O'Reilly, Henry. "Christopher Colles, and the First Proposal of a Telegraph System in the United States". Historical Magazine, Morrisania, N.Y. 1869

O'Reilly, Henry. Settlement in the west: sketches of Rochester; with incidental notices of western New York. (James Brunner, Geneseo, NY, 1984).

Perinton Historical Society. Images of America: Perinton, Fairport, and the Erie Canal (Arcadia Pub. Co., c2001)

Naparsteck, Ruth Rosenberg. Diary of a Young Girl: The Erie Canal in 1822, Vol. LXII, No. 3

Sheriff, Carol. The artificial river: the Erie Canal and the paradox of progress, 1817-1862. (Hill and Wang, c1996)

Shilling, Donovan A. A Towpath Tale: Adventures on the Old Erie Canal, Pancoast Publishing, 2010

Smith, Perry, ed. History of the City of Buffalo and Erie County. D. Mason & Co., Syracuse

Weisberg, Barbara. Talking to the Dead: Kate and Maggie Fox and the Rise of Spiritualism. Harper, 2004

Williams, John Alexander, West Virginia: A History for Beginners (Charleston, WV: Appalachian Editions, 1993)

Wyld, Lionel D. Low Bridge: Folklore and the Erie Canal. Syracuse University Press, 1962.

VIDEO RECORDINGS:

Canal Towns. (WXXI, c2000) VHS; 62 min.—Originally aired on WXXI on September 9, 2000.—Videorecording includes a 19 minute presentation: The Making of Erie Canal Legacy.

Modern Marvels : the Erie Canal. (The History Channel, c2000) VHS; approx. 50 min.—Originally aired on the History Channel on August 14, 2000.

Along the Erie Canal, with Tom Grasso / a film by Pacho Lane. (Ethnoscope Film and Video, c2002) DVD

References

Chapter One: Climate Change

1. http://en.wikipedia.org/wiki/Megafauna
2. http://dinosaurs.about.com/od/otherprehistoriclife/ss/10-Facts-About-the-Saber-Tooth-Tiger.htm
3. http://www.iflscience.com/plants-and-animals/humans-not-climate-change-blame-ice-age-animal-extinction3
4. http://dinosaurs.about.com/od/mesozoicmammals/p/megalonyx.htm
5. https://en.wikipedia.org/wiki/Mastodon5
6. https://nsidc.org/cryosphere/glaciers/gallery/moraines.html
7. http://www.newyorknature.net/IceAge.htm
8. http://www.smithsonianmag.com/history/history-verrazano-narrows-bridge-50-years-after-its-construction-180953032/
9. https://en.wikipedia.org/?title=Clovis_culture

Chapter Two: The First Peoples

1. https://en.wikipedia.org/wiki/Clovis_culture

2. http://bechsed.nylearns.org/pdf/low/Prehistoric

3. http://www.westernny.com/history1.html7

4. http://dictionary.sensagent.com/Lamoka%20Lake/en-en/

5. https://en.wikipedia.org/wiki/Hopewell_tradition

6. http://www.historyforkids.org/learn/northamerica/before1500/history/hopewell.htm

7. https://en.wikipedia.org/wiki/Lenape

8. http://www.newhopepa.com/DelawareRiver/Lenape2.htm

9. https://en.wikipedia.org/wiki/History_of_New_York

10. http://www.warpaths2peacepipes.com/native-american-indians/iroquois-confederacy.htm

11. http://www.indians.org/articles/iroquois-indians.html

12. http://www.newworldencyclopedia.org/entry/Iroquois#Early_History

13. http://www.ushistory.org/us/1d.asp

14. http://www.newworldencyclopedia.org/entry/Tuscarora_ (tribe)

Chapter Three: The Empire State

1. https://en.wikipedia.org/wiki/Giovanni_da_Verrazzano

2. http://www.biography.com/people/giovanni-da-verrazzano-9517737#early-years

3. http://www.huffingtonpost.com/roseanne-colletti/verrazzano-versus-verraza_b_188479.html

4. www.biography.com/people/Jacques-cartier-9240128

5. https://en.wikipedia.org/wiki/Jacques Cartier

6. https://en.wikipedia.org/wiki/Henry_Hudson

7. http://www.history.com/topics/henry-hudson

8. White, G. Edward, Law in American History: Volume 1: From the Colonial Years through the Civil War; Oxford University Press, USA, Feb 20, 2012

References

9. http://www.lettersofnote.com/2011/07/sale-ofmanhattan

10. https://www.onwar.com/aced/chrono/c1600s/yr50/peachtreewar.htm

11. http://indiancountrytodaymedianetwork.com/2013/09/15/native-history-treaty-peach-tree-murder-and-squirrel-smackdown-151278

12. http://www.mountvernon.org/george-washington/french-indian-war/ten-facts-about

13. https://en.wikipedia.org/wiki/Treaty_of_Paris_(1763)

14. https://en.wikipedia.org/wiki/Treaty_of_Fontainebleau_(1762)

15. http://www.sparknotes.com/history/american/revolution/context.html

Chapter Four: Western New York

1. http://blog.mapsofworld.com/2011/08/11/the-french-and-iroqouis-wars-beaver-wars/

2. http://rfester.tripod.com/iroq.html

3. https://en.wikipedia.org/wiki/Seneca_people#Seneca.27s_expanding_influence_and_diplomacy

4. http://www.westernny.com/history1.html

5. http://www.dalecozort.com/alt0798.htm

6. http://www.libraryweb.org/~rochhist/v13_1951/v13i3.pdf

7. https://en.wikipedia.org/wiki/Jesuit_Missions_amongst_the_Huron

8. http://www.oxfordbibliographies.com/view/document/obo-9780199730414/obo-9780199730414-0147.xml

9. https://en.wikipedia.org/wiki/Pequot_people#Pequot_War

10. http://connecticuthistory.org/reckoning-with-the-dutch-the-treaty-of-hartford-1650/

11. http://www.newnetherlandinstitute.org/history-and-heritage/digital-exhibitions/a-tour-of-new-netherland/

12. http://www.fact-index.com/t/tr/treaty_of_hartford.html

13. https://en.wikipedia.org/wiki/Northwest_Indian_War

14. http://financial-dictionary.thefreedictionary.com/scrip

15. https://en.wikipedia.org/wiki/The_Pulteney_Association

16. https://en.wikipedia.org/wiki/Robert_Morris_(financier)

17. http://www.correctionhistory.org/sheriffs/ontario/html/ontariojails_cindysjail01.html

18. http://www.eriecanal.org/UnionCollege/timeline.html

19. http://www.nyheritage.org/collections/holland-land-company-maps

20. http://www.onlinebiographies.info/ny/genesee/ellicott-j.htm

21. http://buffalospree.com/buffalospreemagazine/archives/2004_0506/050604e.html

Chapter Five: A Little Short of Madness

1. https://en.wikipedia.org/wiki/S%C3%A9bastien_Le_Prestre_de_Vauban

2. http://www.fortified-places.com/vauban.html

3. https://en.wikipedia.org/wiki/Cadwallader_Colden

4. http://www.boweryboyshistory.com/2009/11/cadwallader-d-colden-would-grandpa-be_20.html

5. https://en.wikipedia.org/wiki/Christopher_Colles#cite_note-27

6. https://en.wikipedia.org/wiki/Elkanah_Watson

7. https://en.wikipedia.org/wiki/Philip_Schuyler

8. http://www.britannica.com/biography/Robert-Fulton-Americaninventor#ref130832

9. http://www.goodreads.com/book/show/14252215-a-treatise-on-the-improvement-of-canal-navigation

10. https://en.wikipedia.org/wiki/Elizabeth_Schuyler_Hamilton

11. http://www.dmarlin.com/hawley/blog/march2012/index.html

12. http://www.canals.ny.gov/history/history.html

13. https://archive.org/details/pioneerhistoryof00tur

14. https://www.monticello.org/site/research-and-collections/erie-canal

References

15. https://en.wikipedia.org/wiki/History_of_turnpikes_and_canals_in_the_United_States

16. https://en.wikipedia.org/wiki/Jonas_Platt

17. https://en.wikipedia.org/wiki/Erie_Canal commission

18. http://history1800s.about.com/od/canals/a/gallatinreport.htm

19. https://en.wikipedia.org/wiki/Thomas_Eddy

20. http://niagarahistory.org/discovery-center/

21. http://www.canals.ny.gov/history/history.html

22. https://en.wikipedia.org/wiki/Benjamin_Wright

23. http://www.britannica.com/biography/DeWitt-Clinton-American-politician

24. http://www.britannica.com/biography/DeWitt-Clinton-American-politician

25. http://www.eriecanal.org/UnionCollege/Clinton.html

26. http://inthepastlane.com/tag/wedding-of-the-waters/

27. http://www.eriecanal.org/chron.html

28. http://www.eriecanal.org/WeddingoftheWaters

Chapter Six. Salvation

1. https://en.wikipedia.org/wiki/Christian_revival

2. https://en.wikipedia.org/wiki/Second_Great_Awakening

3. https://en.wikipedia.org/wiki/Charles_Grandison_Finney

4. http://en.wikipedia.org/wiki/Age of Enlightenment

5. https://en.wikipedia.org/wiki/Mormonism

6. http://www.gotquestions.org/Latter-Day-Saints.html

7. https://en.wikipedia.org/wiki/Second_work_of_grace

8. https://en.wikipedia.org/wiki/Millerism

9. https://en.wikipedia.org/wiki/Seventh-day_Adventist_Church

10. https://en.wikipedia.org/wiki/Temperance_movement

11. http://www.teachushistory.org/Temperance/forstudents.htm

12. http://www.shakerpedia.com/wiki/Main_Page

Chapter Seven. Without Struggle There's No Progress

1. http://www.frederickdouglass.org/speaking.html

2. http://www.gradesaver.com/narrative-of-the-life-of-frederick-douglass-an-american-slave-written-by-himself/study-guide/summary-chapter-vii

3. http://www.eriecanalway.org/documents/Research_DrJudithWelman_DonPapson.pdf

4. http://www.eiu.edu/eiutps/underground_railroad.php

5. http://freedomcenter.org/content/frederick-douglass

6. http://www.pbs.org/thisfarbyfaith/people/frederick_douglass.html

7. http://www.britannica.com/topic/The-North-Star-American-newspaper

8. http://library.syr.edu/digital/exhibits/g/GerritSmith/dream.htm

9. http://www.examiner.com/article/frederick-douglass-and-john-brown-meet

10. http://www.britannica.com/topic/Harpers-Ferry-Raid

11. https://en.wikipedia.org/wiki/Secret_Six

12. https://annenysec.wordpress.com/2009/01/07/leaders-message-an-enduring-friendship-frederick-douglass-and-susan-b-anthony-february-2009/

13. http://www2.iath.virginia.edu/jbrown/fdlife.html

14. http://plato.stanford.edu/entries/frederick-douglass/#VioSelRe

15. http://blog.oup.com/2007/02/black_history_m4/

16. http://www.math.buffalo.edu/-tubman.

17. https://en.wikipedia.org/wiki/Harriet_Tubman

18. https://en.wikipedia.org/wiki/Uncle_Tom%27s_Cabin#Eva

19. https://www.harrietbeecherstowecenter.org/utc/

References

20. http://www.nps.gov/wori/learn/historyculture/antislavery-connection.htm

Chapter Eight. Ain't I a Women?

1. http://www.newworldencyclopedia.org/entry/Charles_Grandison_Finney
2. http://www.christianitytoday.com/ch/1988/issue20/2006.html?start=2
3. http://www.pbs.org/godinamerica/people/charles-finney.html
4. http://www.crookedlakereview.com/books/saints_sinners/martin7.html
5. https://www.apstudynotes.org/us-history/topics/reform-crusades/
6. https://en.wikipedia.org/wiki/Seneca_Falls_Convention
7. http://faculty.uml.edu/sgallagher/SenecaFalls.htm
8. http://www.co.seneca.ny.us/wp-content/uploads/2014/11/Birth-of-the-Womens-Rights-Movement-in-Seneca-County-pdf
9. https://en.wikipedia.org/wiki/Elizabeth_Cady_Stanton
10. http://trilogy.brynmawr.edu/speccoll/quakersandslavery/commentary/themes/radical_quakerwomen.php
11. https://en.wikipedia.org/wiki/Universal_suffrage
12. https://en.wikipedia.org/wiki/Declaration_of_Sentiments
13. https://en.wikipedia.org/wiki/Lucretia_Mott
14. http://www.womenhistoryblog.com/2013/10/amy-kirby-post.html
15. http://faculty.history.wisc.edu/sommerville/367/367-072.htm
16. https://en.wikipedia.org/wiki/Fox_sisters
17. https://en.wikipedia.org/wiki/Spiritualism
18. http://www.biography.com/people/sojourner-truth
19. https://en.wikipedia.org/wiki/Sojourner_Truth
20. http://www.notablebiographies.com/St-Tr/Truth-Sojourner.html#ixzz3oJBnCGRj
21. http://www.freethought-trail.org/profile.php?By=Person&Page=38

Chapter Nine. The Psychic Highway

1. http://www.eriecanalway.org/explore_things-to-do_erie-canal-trail.htm

2. http://roc.democratandchronicle.com/article/20080602/NEWS0204/806020321/Rochester-s-religious-revival-had-far-reach

3. https://en.wikipedia.org/wiki/Whitney_Cross

4. https://en.wikipedia.org/wiki/Carl_Carmer

5. http://carlcarmer.blogspot.com/

6. https://en.wikipedia.org/wiki/Oneida_Community

7. http://patrickdoud.com/2012/05/26/the-publick-universal-friend-mary-tammer-

8. http://www.spiritdaily.net/niagara2.htm

9. http://www.sunypress.edu/p-6033-upstate-cauldron.aspx

10. http://www.masonwinfield.com/

11. http://cnypr.org/

12. http://theshadowlands.net/ghost/

13. http://www.o-books.com/authors/madis-senner

Appendix A

The Seneca's Rise to Power

Historical evidence of the Seneca's rising scope and power in the lower Catskill regions of Sullivan and Ulster Counties includes, in part:

- 1657-1658: Seneca diplomats visit Dutch colonial officials in New Amsterdam, New York.

- 1659-1660: The Seneca intervene in the First Esopus War between the Dutch and Esopus natives near what is now Kingston. The Seneca chief urged Peter Stuyvesant (governor of New Amsterdam) to end the bloodshed and "return the captured Esopus savages."

- 1675: After a decade of war between the Iroquois and the Andaste/Susquehannock, the Seneca vanquish them as one of their last remaining enemies and assimilate their survivors into the Seneca and Cayuga tribes.

- 1720 to the 1750s: The Seneca resettle and assimilate the Munsee into the Iroquois Confederacy.

- 1756: The Iroquois Confederacy settles the Munsee in present day Corning (Seneca territory).

- Beginning of the 18th century: Despite French military campaigns, Seneca power remains intact as they begin to ally themselves with the British and Dutch against France.

- 1760: The Seneca help the British capture Fort Niagara during the Seven Years' War.

Appendix B
Treaties

The Treaty of Hartford included 2 earlier historic agreements prior to the Treaty of 1786. They are the Treaty of 1638, the Treaty of 1650.

The Treaty of 1638 assigned the spoils of the Pequot War.

The Pequot tribe was of Algonquin descent and inhabited much of what is now Connecticut. Long-standing ill will between English colonists and Pequot natives resulted in open warfare (The Pequot War) in 1637 when a Pequot soldier killed an Englishman whom he had mistaken for Dutch. The Pequot fought against an alliance of colonists in Massachusetts Bay; Plymouth, Massachusetts, Saybrook, Connecticut; and their native allies, the Narragansett and the Mohegan. This was called the Pequot War. The Pequot were defeated and virtually eliminated.

The Treaty of 1638 officially assigned the remaining Pequot population.

- Several hundred were taken as captives; some of whom were sold into slavery in the West Indies or were placed as household servants.

- Other survivors were equally divided among the Narrangansett and Mohegan tribes; with lesser numbers awarded to tribes on

Long Island.

- Pequot lands were distributed among towns along the Connecticut River—the longest in New England.

- No future Pequot towns or settlements would be allowed.

- The Pequot language and name was outlawed. Survivors would be referred to as Mohegan or Narragansett.

The Treaty of 1650 settled boundary disputes between the English and the Dutch.

Representatives from New Netherlands (Dutch) and New England (English) met in Hartford, Connecticut to settle boundary disputes; beginning with that of the Dutch trading post (the House of Hope), established in 1633 on the Connecticut River. Three years later a Dutch party, under the direction of Thomas Hooker, established what he deemed the location of Hartford to be. Throughout the 1630s and 1640s, English settlers had haphazardly established new towns up and down the river and along its coast.

On October 12, 1650, the colonial representatives signed a treaty provisionally relinquishing Dutch claims to the Connecticut River Valley. Conflicts continued. It wasn't until 1674 that the Dutch finally ceded the New Netherlands settlement to the English. New Netherland extended from Albany, New York through other areas of the state; to New York, New Jersey, Pennsylvania, Maryland, Connecticut and Delaware.

The Treaty of 1786 divided Western New York land between New York and Massachusetts.

The original colonial charters of New York and Massachusetts both described their boundaries as "extending westward to the Pacific Ocean", using coastal rivers as their measurements. This vague description resulted in both states claiming the same land.

The land in dispute was essentially all of western New York State, from Seneca Lake, to the Niagara River and Lake Erie; north to Lake Ontario and south to the Pennsylvania border.

Both states agreed to divide their rights to the land as follows:

Appendix B

- All (about 6 million acres) of the land would become part of and governed by New York State.
- Massachusetts received "preemption rights" or the title to the land and the right to sell it. Today, this is also known as "first option to buy".
- The treaty also provided that Massachusetts had the right to sell or "assign" its preemptive rights, which it did in 1788. Massachusetts sold all 6 million acres and the title to land speculators Oliver Phelps and Nathaniel Gorham for 1 million dollars, using the money to recover debts incurred during the Revolutionary War.

After the Revolutionary War, The Treaty of Canandaigua (1794) was signed in Canandaigua, New York between President George Washington and the Grand Council of the Six Nations (The Iroquois Nation) which was represented by a contingent of 50 sachems and war chiefs of the Cayuga, Mohawk, Oneida, Onondaga, Seneca and Tuscarora tribes. Timothy Pickering, an official agent for the president, was also present.

The treaty put an end to New York State's intermittent illegal land transactions with Native Americans through the late 1780s and early 1790s. The formation of treaties and outright land purchases were first deemed illegal under Article 9 of the Articles of Confederation—an agreement among the 13 original states of the United States of America, which served as the nation's first constitution. Subsequently, illegal land transactions were also outlawed under the Commerce Clause of the constitution, which stated, "...the United States Congress shall have power to regulate commerce with foreign Nations, and among the several States, and with the Indian Tribes."

Concerned that nefarious New York land deals would prompt Indian tribes to join a pan-Indian military alliance in defense of the Ohio River valley—a movement led by powerful Shawnee leader, Tecumseh—the United States entered into the Treaty of Canandaigua.

On September 15, 1797, the Treaty of Big Tree was signed between the United States and the Seneca Nation, individually, who relinquished their right to the majority of their traditional homeland in New York State; particularly ceding their rights to all the land west of the Genesee River. Previously, in 1788, the Iroquois Nation had sold rights to their land—between Seneca Lake and the Genesee River—in what is known as the Phelps and Gorham purchase.

The treaty is noteworthy as it opened up the remaining territory west of the Genesee River for American settlement.

Appendix C

The Founding of Buffalo: It Takes a Village

The establishment of the Village of Buffalo (1801-1832) would progress at a relatively slowly pace until the War of 1812, at which time it functioned as a "military resort."

Buffalo's 1832 City Directory states, "In December, 1813, the place was entered by the British and Indians, and every building but two was burnt. Many citizens were taken as captives to Montreal and most of the rest fled to avoid capture. The loss and destruction of property was borne by the individuals more than the village itself as Buffalo had yet to become incorporated with the attendant municipal responsibilities and facilities."

Getting Buffalo back up on its economic feet was a grueling, slow-moving process, especially impeded by the lack of accessible transportation to trading markets. In 1819 talk of the impending "Grand Canal" gathered momentum and brightened Buffalo's prospects. It also drew more settlers to the area. An exact western destination for the canal had not yet been confirmed, but Buffalo was ready.

Buffalo or Black Rock?

Great physical labor and a $12,000 loan was obtained from the state and through private donations to make the mouth of Buffalo Creek navigable, so that vessels would not have to dock at Black Rock, Buffalo's earliest commercial rival.

Essentially, the mouth of the harbor was relocated further south, according to a clever plan by Samuel Wilkeson, to avoid a persistent sand bar which continually reformed, despite many efforts to eradicate it. The Erie Canal would only help Buffalo if ships could conveniently reach it.

The reconstruction process was almost finished with Mother Nature interfered. Torrential rains threatened destroy all that had already been successfully completed. Wilkeson appealed to the villagers to help redirect the waters of the soggy land around Buffalo Creek. Their efforts paid off, as the creek cooperated and flushed tons of earth into Lake Erie and Buffalo Harbor miraculously took shape.

The competition between Buffalo and Black Rock was on! General Peter Porter, of Black Rock was an eloquent statesman who naturally advocated for the Black Rock location. Buffalo, however, had the advantage of being situated higher on Lake Erie. Black Rock sat on the Niagara River at a substantially lower elevation.

Oh, the Suspense!

Porter and Wilkeson each "campaigned" for their respective locations as the potential home of the Erie Canal. Porter had a way with words, but Wilkeson had facts: he had drawn up the plans; conceived of and implemented the idea to redesign the water flow and understood the practicality of not tampering with the construction that had already gone forward. Besides, the only way to excavate ground, at the time, was by using manual labor. This would not only prolong the time-frame of the project; it would also become more costly.

In 1822, the canal commissioners left the Eagle Tavern one day—and the area—after lengthy deliberations, giving the impression that Buffalo had the edge in the debate.

The wait was agonizing, but in the winter of the same year a decision was announced. Buffalo would, indeed, become the site of the Erie Canal!

The Village of Buffalo had been incorporated in 1822, with a government administered by a president and board of trustees. In 1825, it received federal monies in compensation for the destruction sustained during the 1812 War. It also saw the completion of the Erie Canal.

Buffalo gained prominence at lightning speed. Wharves and storehouses immediately appeared along the harbor and the city soon became the largest grain handling and shipping port in the world. The "Grand Canal" was a prosperous reality as the "gateway to the West".

By 1832, Buffalo was bustling with banks, insurance companies, and water works projects which replaced "Water Johns", peddlers with a horse cart toting potable water. Local breweries sprang up, beginning a tradition of producing home-brewed lager beers, which would continue into the 1970s.

Buffalo's future was bright. On April 20, 1832, Governor Enos T. Throop approved the charter of the City of Buffalo.

The Founding of Syracuse

In its infancy, Syracuse—like Rochester and Buffalo—was a small village. It was situated on the south end of Onondaga Lake. In 1654, Jesuit missionary priest, Fr. Simon LeMoyne, discovered large salty brine deposits in the water, which would give the lake its nickname: "Salt Lake". This site would become the original location of the city of Syracuse—with a plentiful natural resource that would put it on the economic trading map.

Grains of Salt:

- In 1777, the first settler to arrive was Ephraim Webster who quickly took advantage of the salt resource and opened a trading post. He was followed by others who also profited in this way. Commercial salt production flourished through the early 1900s. The process of accessing brine wells that tapped into halite beds in Salina shale deposits, were developed near Tully, New York. Flowing brine from Tully was the source of the "salty springs" located along the shores of Onondaga Lake.

- In 1800, state assemblyman Comfort Tyler secured a charter for the Seneca Turnpike Company. With $100,000 he initiated the construction of a turnpike toll road on the old state road between Utica and Canandaigua. The road was finished in 1812 and improved communications between people in the eastern and western areas.

- Also in 1800, attorney Joshua Forman moved to Onondaga Hollow with his wife, his father, and his four brothers. He opened

a law office in the village. He also leased a tract of land 40 miles north around Oswego Falls and built a gristmill, which started settlement of that area.
- In 1801, 6 villages vied for the title of county seat. Onondaga Hill was chosen.
- The village of Salina was incorporated in 1824; Syracuse followed in 1825.
- In 1829 the county seat was relocated to Syracuse.
- In 1847 Syracuse received its city charter.
- Railways began to appear in New York State in the 1830s. The initial lines were established first in the eastern portion of the state and in 1838 the Auburn and Syracuse Railroad was put into action. The Syracuse and Utica Railroad opened in 1839.

The opening of the Erie Canal in 1825 boosted Syracuse's productivity and popularity even higher. Low shipping rates were insured due to an increase in the city's salt production and distribution, which at the time of the Civil War, peaked at 8 million bushels annually. But, at the end of the war, Syracuse's salt manufacturing operations were threatened by competition from Michigan and Canada, causing businesses to explore other manufacturing options.

In 1861, Ernest Solvay developed an ammonia-soda process for the production of soda ash (anhydrous sodium carbonate or a rare chemical called natrite), taken from brine wells in the southern end of the Tully valley, and limestone.

By 1884, this alternate method of yielding a salt product was being conducted at the first Solvay Process Company plant, which was built on the southwestern shore of Onondaga Lake. Unfortunately, the Syracuse Solvay Plant was the model for the large chemical industry complex, Allied Signal, which would eventually cause the extreme pollution of the lake.

The Homestead Act of 1862 was signed into law by President Abraham Lincoln allowing anyone who had never taken up arms against the United States government (including freed slaves and women), was 21 years of age or older, and/or the head of a family, could file an application to claim a federal land grant.

In 1876, David Cook was the first settler to work his granted land. He plowed in the spring of 1876 and sowed grain in the fall. Joseph Bodily built

Appendix C

the first log cabin in the area in 1877 on 80 acres of "homesteaded" land.

The first settlers of Syracuse found ways to turn their natural environment into profits.

By 1884, the extended Hooper Canal carried water from the Weber River, encouraging homesteaders to develop property near the shore. Grass and hay grew in abundance. The dairy cow business also flourished, prompting a group of farmers to build a cheese factory. Land was carefully cultivated for fruit farming. Artesian wells with cement holding ponds provided irrigation for acres of apple, peach, pear and plum planting. By the turn of the century, Syracuse was the largest fruit producer in Davis County. From 1893 on, new row crops were introduced, including sugar beets, potatoes, tomatoes, peas and the Syracuse Canning Factory appeared.

The first general store was built by Isaac Barton in 1888. In 1891, the Syracuse post office was commissioned with John Coles as its first postmaster. After the L.D.S. Church established a Syracuse Ward in the center of town in 1895, a central school appeared; an amusement hall and other noteworthy businesses, such as Syracuse Mercantile, Rampton's Blacksmith Shop, Homers' Barbershop, the Kaysville Canning Factory, and the Bountiful Lumber Yard.

The first New York State Fair was held in Syracuse in 1841. It had no permanent home for many years, but in 1890 it moved back to Syracuse, to stay. In 1849, a device very similar to the Ferris wheel was put into operation for the first time at the New York State Fair in Syracuse.

The Erie Canal Museum still stands in the original 1850 Weighlock Building in Syracuse, where canal boats were weighed as they passed through the center of the city during the canal's heyday.

Follow the Yellow Brick Road... to Syracuse?

L. Frank Baum (1856 - 1919), author of the *Wonderful Wizard of Oz*, lived in Syracuse at 1 Rust Street when he was a boy. Most storytellers draw on their own life experiences and travels and incorporate them into their works. Was Baum inspired by what he saw and experienced in Syracuse?

Is the book's "gardens of Roselawn" a reference to the many fruits and flowers of home? The "plank road" sounds familiar. And, who might the "Cardiff Giant" be? Or, Professor C.C. Coe?

And, how did they end up in Oz?

Appendix D
Frederick Douglass' Life as a Slave

Douglass' first master was a man named Anthony—Captain Anthony—who sailed commercially on the Chesapeake Bay. Anthony was superintendent or "overseer of the overseers" at the huge home plantation of Colonel Edward Lloyd.

Anthony's second-in-command was a Mr. Plummer, a mean, foul-mouthed drunk who took great pleasure in whipping slaves—particularly women—until the leather slid haphazardly into the bloody grooves they'd just manufactured.

Colonel Lloyd had 2 sons, Andrew and Richard; and a daughter, Lucretia, who was married to Captain Thomas Auld. They all lived in 1 house on the plantation, north of Easton in Talbot County, Maryland. Lloyd also owned about 20 smaller farms. It was reported that he had about 1,000 slaves. Douglass spent 2 years of his childhood there.

Basic "Comforts"

Slaves from the outlying farms received their allotments of food and yearly pieces of clothing at Lloyd's outlying farms. Men and women received 8-pounds of pork, or fish, and one bushel of cornmeal, which was to last a month. Douglass was not among the regularly allowanced. His food staple was "mush"—coarse boiled corn meal, literally served in a communal trough.

Slaves wore articles of clothing made of "Negro cloth"—coarse unbleached cotton. Their yearly clothing allotment consisted of 2 shirts, 2 pair of trousers, 1 jacket, 1 pair of stockings (socks) and 1 pair of shoes. The cost of all was less than $7.

Children too young to work in the field were not given shoes, stockings, jackets or trousers. They received just 2 long shirts per year. If these became worn, the children went naked, no matter what the season, until they were entitled to new ones. Children from 7 to 10 years-of-age fell into this category, including Douglass.

There were no beds in the slaves' quarters. Some adult men and women may have had 1 blanket. Men, women, and older children were so exhausted at the end of the day that they literally slept wherever they sat. Besides completing their daily work, slaves were responsible for maintaining their own surroundings; washing clothing, sewing and mending it, and cooking meals.

Early each morning they were wakened and summoned to the field by the blare of the boss' horn. This was the routine of the aptly named Mr. Severe, who stood doorway of the slaves' quarters holding a cowhide whip and a hickory stick, which he would use on anyone late to the field.

When Mr. Severe died, Mr. Hopkins took his place. He was not prone to "extraordinary demonstrations of cruelty"; and seemed to take no pleasure in whipping the slaves. He was called a "good" overseer by them. For these reasons, he too, was soon replaced by Mr. Austin Gore, who met and surpassed Colonel Lloyd's expectations regarding the hideous treatment of slaves.

Mr. Austin Gore—the most dreaded of all the overseers—eventually replaced Mr. Severe. Douglass described him as "proud, ambitious and persevering"; also "artful, cruel and obdurate". He interpreted a simple look, gesture or sound from a slave as reason for immediate physical punishment. He particularly delighted in ordering slaves into the most debasing posture, of literally crouching and cowering at his feet.

On one occasion, an old slave named Demby jumped into a stream to soothe his bloody gashes after one of Gore's whippings. Gore grabbed his gun, saying he'd count to 3, expecting Demby to get out of the water. The man remained trembling in the stream, as Gore shot him in the head.

Killing a slave—or any person of color—was not considered a crime in Talbot County, Maryland, by the judicial system or by the public. Even little white children repeated the phrase they'd frequently heard their parents recite: "It was worth a half-cent to kill a 'nigger', and a half-cent to bury one."

The Psychic Highway

Learning to Read: "Believe in Yourself":

Douglass was just 7 or 8-years-old when he left Colonel Lloyd's plantation for Baltimore to live and serve in the home of Hugh Auld, brother to Thomas Auld, Lloyd's son-in-law. "I shall never forget the ecstasy", wrote Douglass. "I left with the highest hopes of future happiness."

This shift to a proper home among kinder people was a sign from God; a prayer answered, for which he would be eternally grateful. His job would be looking after the needs of young Thomas Auld, who called Douglass, "Freddy".

Douglass' new mistress, Sophia Auld, was the most welcomed surprise in his new environment. Thomas Auld, Sr.'s wife never before had a slave under her personal control.

"She was entirely unlike any other white woman I had ever seen. I could not approach her as I was accustomed to approach other white ladies. My early instruction was all out of place. The crouching servility, usually so acceptable a quality in a slave, did not answer when manifested toward her. Her favor was not gained by it; she seemed to be disturbed by it. Her face was made of heavenly smiles and her voice of tranquil music", recalled Douglass.

It was Sophia Auld who taught him to read, in what constituted a rather odd set of circumstances. Here was a young, grateful mulatto boy learning to read and write language for the first time, under the tutelage of a good white woman who, for the first time in her life, had a slave in service.

But, just as "Freddy" was progressing in his studies, Mr. Auld forbade his wife to continue, raging that she was breaking the law in teaching a slave to read. Learning how to read, he said, would "spoil the best nigger in the world", forever making him "unfit" to be a slave.

A light went on in Douglass' head, as he processed Mr. Auld's reasoning and began to understand the complexities of slavery for the white man. Education on the parts of slaves, even at its absolute minimum, would challenge, if not put a fearful damper on slavery. And worse, it might even place a lowly black person in the same (or higher) intellectual arena as a white man. "I now understood what had been to me a most perplexing difficulty —the white man's power to enslave the black man. (This realization) was a grand achievement, and I prized it highly. From that moment, I understood the pathway of slavery to freedom", wrote Douglass.

Almost immediately, Mrs. Auld became impassioned with replicating the

Appendix D

same hateful behaviors of her husband."Nothing seemed to make her more angry than to see me with a newspaper", Douglass recorded. The life lesson she learned was that education and slavery were wildly incompatible.

Bread for Brainpower: "Take Advantage of Every Opportunity":

Douglass followed one of his most important life rules—"take advantage of every opportunity"—in his quest for learning. He first went about making friends with the white boys he met in the street and "converted them into teachers". He'd quickly accomplish an errand, then seek out boys his age and ask them to teach him to read from a book he'd carried with him.

Douglass bartered chunks of bread he'd taken from his home for these precious lessons. Often, he'd talk to them about his life as a slave and wish he could be as free as these young boys. Douglass also took advantage of "borrowing" the school copy-books of his young master, Thomas, to study and re-write the words he found there.

At around age 12, he began reading what became his favorite book, "The Columbian Orator"—a textbook on grammar and rhetoric by Caleb Bingham—which included a story of a slave who had run away from his master 3 times. In an unexpected ending, the master was impressed with the slave's arguments for freedom and agreed to voluntarily emancipate him.

In the same book, Douglass read Richard Sheridan's speeches on Catholic emancipation and others by orators William Pitt, George Washington, Charles James Fox and Cicero. His attachment to the content of their speeches would further Douglass' deep love of liberty and hatred of oppression. It became clear to Douglass in newspaper stories that the discussion of the abolition of slavery in the District of Columbia and other states was something synonymous with freedom.

When Douglass helped two men working on a boat at the city wharf, they asked him if he was a slave for life. He thought their conversation might have been a trap, and pretended not to pay attention. But, he heard it. One of the men encouraged him to try to escape to the north.

The Psychic Highway

The Division of Property

His first master, Captain Anthony, died about 5 years after Douglass had been sent to Baltimore. He left no will, so it was necessary to perform an evaluation as to the worth of his property, which would be divided between his remaining heirs; son, Andrew and daughter, Lucretia. Douglass was "bequeathed" to Lucretia, who decided that he'd stay in Baltimore. There, his master had succumbed to excessive inebriation and his mistress, to angry tirades. Ultimately, he was sent to live with his young master, Thomas, who lived about 78-miles away from Baltimore.

In his *Narrative*, Douglass wrote," I have now reached a period of my life when I can give dates. I left Baltimore... in the sloop Amanda with Captain Edward Dodson... and went to live with Master Thomas Auld, in March, 1832." On his trip, he paid particular attention to the north-easterly direction steamboats took on their way to Philadelphia and was more determined than ever to run away, waiting only for a "favorable opportunity".

Master Thomas' Religion

Douglass learned that the young Master Thomas he knew years earlier in Baltimore had adopted the same cruel mentality and actions toward slaves as his parents. Both Thomas and Rowena, his wife, made sure that food was routinely withheld from their slaves. Over time, the practice among masters of not feeding slaves well enough, had diminished. It was not considered "respectable" to do so. Thomas, however, did not follow suit.

Douglass would deliberately let his master's horse run away, so he'd have to chase it down to Rowena's family farm, where he'd be assured of getting something to eat. Thomas would often tell Douglass that city living had ruined him for "every purpose".

In the summer of 1832, Thomas and Rowena attended a Methodist camp revival. One might think that this would result in more kindly treatment toward their slaves, but it only strengthened their usual behavior. "He found religious sanction and support for his slaveholding cruelty," wrote Douglass," while he (Thomas) maintained an intense pretension to piety." They welcomed preachers into their home where they were well-fed as the slaves starved.

Appendix D

A Defining Moment of Hoodoo

As a final effort to break Douglass of what Thomas considered insolence, he sent him to Edward Covey, a poor, crude farmer known for being the consummate "slave-breaker". Covey was hard-working, but expected superhuman results from slaves. He, too, claimed to be religious, using his beliefs to "tame" slaves.

Douglass' life experiences were never harder, more dehumanizing and abasing than those he knew under Covey's control. Yet, when his desperation and anger reached their peak, Douglass turned to a source of inner strength to see him through a physical fight between them. It was a marathon of muscle and intellectual cunning—and an episode that convinced Covey to never again lay a hand upon this young slave.

African folk beliefs known as hoodoo came in handy for Douglass in this horrendous fight to the finish. Hoodoo does not derive from organized religion, but refers to the practice of supporting thought and/or action with a distinct kind of spiritual inspiration, empowerment, "karma" or "pay-back", specific to the moment and for the purpose for which it is channeled.

The concept was originally brought to America by African slaves who spoke a language called "Hausa", in which the term "hu'du'ba" means "arouse resentment (and) produce retribution". Hoodoo is something used to invoke or call up the result of one's desires, predominately in times of distress or anger.

In his confrontation with Covey, Douglass seemed protected and guided by this kind of overwhelming aura or strength, which most likely surprised both participants.

In African American spiritual folklore, hoodoo can co-exist with organized religion, such as Christianity. And, if hoodoo should negatively manifest itself against someone who has committed a moral wrong, the overriding belief was that God, too, had a hand in willing the event to happen. Douglass' religion or personal faith was augmented by the spiritual nuances of black culture and its African religious roots.

Escape to Freedom

Through his teen years Douglass worked among free black men as a ship caulker in the Fells Point shipyard in Baltimore. His relationship with the Aulds had matured into something more positive. Time and sensibilities weighed heavily on Thomas Auld, Sr. and Sophia Auld, who eventually supported Douglass in his fight against the oppression of slavery.

During this time, he met a free black woman named Anna Murray, who encouraged his escape and helped plan its details. His fellow workers gave him a seaman uniform, identifying him as a free black shipyard worker. One of them also gave him identification papers proving this status.

Frederick Douglass left Baltimore on September 3, 1838, traveling by train to Maryland, crossing the Susquehanna River by ferry, then boarding another train to Wilmington, Delaware. He traveled by steamboat to Philadelphia, and finally to New York City, where he used the last name "Johnson" to avoid recapture. He and Anna married there.

He learned that "colored persons" were being hired as ship caulkers at the New Bedford, Massachusetts pier, as a result of the mounting anti-slavery effort in the north. He and Anna moved to New Bedford, where it took just 3 days for him to be hired "stowing a sloop with a load of oil". "It was new, dirty, hard work for me; but I went at it with a glad heart and a willing hand. I was now my own master", he wrote. He again changed his name—for the final time—to Frederick Douglass.

He and Anna lived with the Johnson family in New Bedford, Massachusetts in a house which has been preserved and restored as a National Historic Landmark, prominent in the role of the nation's Underground Railroad. Husband and wife, Nathan and Polly Johnson, were among the city's best known abolitionists in the 19th century.

Preacher, Orator, Abolitionist:
"Use the Power of the Spoken and Written Language to Effect Positive Change for Yourself and Society"

The one sustaining tool Douglass shared with other slaves was teaching them to read. Prior to successfully achieving his escape, he secretly organized a rudimentary Sunday school for other slaves.

"I held my Sabbath school at the house of a free colored man... (with) over 40 scholars... ardently desiring to learn", he reported. "I look back at those Sundays with an amount of pleasure not to be expressed. They were great days to my soul", he wrote.

As a free man, he began attending lectures at New York's American Anti-

Appendix D

Slavery Society (1833-1870), founded by noted abolitionists William Lloyd Garrison and Arthur Tappan. Most of its leaders were white and eager to give black abolitionists opportunities to be heard. Douglass became a key leader of the group. Members included figures in the women's suffrage movement: Susan B. Anthony, Elizabeth Cady Stanton, Lucretia Mott and others.

In New Bedford, Douglass became a leader in the local black community as an ordained, licensed minister at the African Methodist Episcopal Zion Church. He began speaking out against the American Colonization Society, founded in 1816 by Reverend Robert Finley, a Presbyterian minister from New Jersey. The goal of the society was to "assist" free blacks in emigration to Africa, "the land of their fathers". Finley believed that blacks would never fully integrate into American society and viewed colonization in Africa as a charitable measure. He thought it would also bring an end to slavery.

As long as blacks remained in America, Finley maintained that their presence would only threaten its national well-being and harm the white quality of life. Removing blacks from American society, he advised, would save Americans from eventual inter-racial marriages and having the burden of providing for poor blacks. Douglass infused his abolitionist efforts with the opinion that the United States was the true home of black Americans.

Some of Douglass' anti-colonization essays were published in the *Liberator*, a respected anti-slavery publication, which brought him to the attention of major abolitionist leaders. After attending a convention of the Bristol Massachusetts Anti-Slavery Society in Nantucket in 1841, he became a colleague of William Lloyd Garrison and a frequent lecturer for the Massachusetts society.

Appendix E

The French and Indian War

Washington Surrenders in Counter Attack:
The Battle of Great Meadow

Captain Louis Coulon de Villiers, Ensign Jumonville's brother, was ordered by his French commander at Fort Duquesne to attack Washington's forces near Great Meadows. Coulon de Villiers set out to do this with 600 French soldiers, a group of Canadian soldiers and 100 native ally warriors.

Washington's forces had been severely depleted in the first battle, leaving only 300 available men. They had taken cover in a small, rickety wooden fort—Fort Necessity—which was conspicuously situated in the middle of the meadow, making it extremely vulnerable if attacked from the surrounding wooded hills.

The French made their move on July 1, 1754. When they opened fire on the fort, Washington agreed to surrender. It would be the only time he would do so. Whether it was the pouring rain and soaking wet conditions that day or that the terms of the surrender were written in French and insufficiently translated, Washington did not notice upon signing it, one particular clause in the document which accused him of "assassinating" Ensign Jumonville.

Appendix E

The Battle of Monongahela

In the spring of 1755, Washington was appointed as an aide-de-camp to Major General Edward Braddock who was to lead a force of 2,100 British regulars (foot soldiers) and 500 colonial soldiers to Fort Duquesne to overthrow the French stronghold. Moving his men and weapons over the dense Allegheny Mountains was a huge challenge. Washington knew the terrain and expertly maneuvered them through it.

As they reached the Monongahela River, they were pummeled by the French. Thirteen-hundred of Braddock's men were killed, as were most of the senior British officers, including Braddock, himself. Washington sprang into action and quickly re-established order. During the ensuing battle, 2 horses were shot from underneath him as he charged into the fray and his coat was ripped apart by 4 musket balls. He was in charge, remaining focused and helping those who survived to safer ground.

The British loss was great, yet Washington was praised as "the hero of Monongahela" by Governor Dinwiddie who promoted him to Colonel in command of the 1,200-man Virginia Regiment.

The Capture of Fort Duquesne:
The Forbes Expedition (1757-1758)

With 2 failed efforts to take Fort Duquesne behind him, Washington commanded the Virginia Regiment as an attachment to Brigadier General John Forbes' expedition against the fort, from 1757 to1758.

Forbes' militia consisted of 2,000 British Regulars and 5,000 colonial soldiers, with whom he chose to head westward to the French fort, rather than pursue the southerly route strongly recommended by Washington.

Washington's forces had been operating from Fort Ligonier in Pennsylvania in an area east of the French fort. On November 24, 1758 Washington's Virginia Regiment finally succeeded in taking the French stronghold; destroying and burning it to the ground until it was nothing but smoking ruins. The British now controlled this coveted region of the Ohio River.

Ebenezer "Indian" Allan: An 18th Century Walter Mitty

E benezer "Indian" Allan was—for lack of a better and/or polite word—a character! In familiar terms, we could call him a scam artist, an imposter, a charlatan, or a very good actor. The bottom line, however, was Indian Allan's heart and sliding allegiances were always justified—by him. And, like the charming Walter Mitty character, he was convincing in his efforts and self-assigned roles.

If Indian Allan were here today, he'd surely want to tell his story, himself. What might he say, in a fictionalized version?

~

I was born on the 17th day of September in 1752 in Morris Township, New Jersey, and I died on the 13th day of April in 1813 in a place called Delaware Township, way up in Canada.

I've lived most of my life in the wild, but I've always been for the underdog. I consider myself a friend of the Seneca Indians and the Iroquois people. I guess we trusted each other.

I was down there in Pennsylvania around 1777 when something called to me to join the Loyalist unit of the war regiment under Major John Butler. They called his rogue brigade Butler's Rangers. Because of my good relationship with the Indians, I was sent to the Indian Department in 1781 and the following year... (now, make sure no one else is listening)... I became a Loyalist spy (can you imagine that), assigned to the Genesee River area in western New York.

That was a hard job, but sweet Mary Jemison made my stay easier. They called her the "White Woman of the Genesee"; the Indians adopted her when she was a little girl. I lived with her, there, through my days of "espionage".

Between 1782 and 1783 I moved to what would be called Mount Morris, after that rich American man with money for the war, Robert Morris. It was winter and it was cold! I needed to provide for myself, so I started farming and trading my goods. I was a Lieutenant with the Indian Department by then... but the war was coming to an end and they started letting men go. I was one of them. That's what I got for siding with the British against these new Americans.

I was really laid low. I asked myself, "What can ya' do, Indian, to help the American cause, this time? And, my Iroquois friends?" I decided to show 'em something they could see with their own eyes, to let them know that I could bring about a sincere peace.

I knew I was taking a big chance, but I snuck into a big Indian village and into the chief's longhouse. I looked around for something important to signify "peace". Ah! There it was! A beauty of a wampum belt! When the American Indian Commissioner sees this, he'll believe it means the Iroquois want to live peacefully among the Americans and my Indian brothers will honor the gesture! I felt that if I could live for another few hundred years, I may even have a shot at the Nobel Peace Prize!

Ebenezer's Plight

Well, I spoke too soon. The British were still very mad at me and sent out a party of soldiers to hunt me down. They found me alright and threw me in prison! Since the end of the war, I was treated cruelly and inhumanly. There I was, robbed, stripped, plundered and imprisoned like some common criminal! And, for what? I was doing the right thing! For 10 months I was shifted from prison to prison; from Fort Niagara in New York, then up to Montreal in Canada and to Cataraqui, in Ontario.

THE PSYCHIC HIGHWAY

I'm a Lover When I'm Not a Fighter

"Polygamy reduced to a fine art with a successful audacity
that might excite the admiration of a Mormon elder."

I made my way back to the Genesee country I knew and loved... and
to the women I knew and loved. I took Sally as my Indian wife by
blessing of my Indian brothers. She gave me two daughters, Chloe and
Mary. Around 1789 we canoed down river to a 474-acre farmstead in
what would become Scottsville. Some will say the Seneca gave this
land to me; others say—because there is a deed to prove it—that I
bought it for 200 pounds in Massachusetts money from a man named
Israel Chapin.

A Mr. Chapman came our way on his way to Niagara. His
daughter, Lucy, accompanied him. He seemed to like me... and so did
Lucy. I wasn't intending for it to happen, but Mr. Chapman gave me
her hand in marriage. Lucy stayed and her father went west—alone.

Someone would write that I 'combined the lasciviousness of a
Turk with the bloodthirstiness of a savage' in my life with Lucy and
Sally and my children... and others. Social conventions meant nothing
to me. Yes, during my years in Delaware Township I was surrounded
by many "wives" and more children.

I was living happily and was not aware of the big meeting (the
Buffalo Creek Indian Council of 1787 or Treaty of Big Tree) with Mr.
Oliver Phelps and Mr. Nathaniel Gorham and the Iroquois chiefs. The
white men wanted a large portion of land west of the Genesee. My
brothers insisted that their Great Spirit wanted no white men west of
the great river. Mr. Phelps said the Seneca needed a grist mill to grind
maize just as white settlers needed one to ground wheat. A mill would
ease women's work.

Mr. Phelps said he needed—and got—288-square-miles west of
the Genesee approximately 12 miles wide, and stretching 24-miles
from Avon to Lake Ontario. He became owner of the largest mill lot
in the world.

The grist mill needed an operator and I was the person for the job!
I was given the 100-acre site with the understanding that I would build

and run the mill. A small, natural island in the river helped channel water to the mill and some 3 and 4-foot waterfalls gave enough drop in water level to turn the water wheels to fuel a sawmill and a grist mill.

I brought in a saw blade and managed to connect it to a makeshift water wheel to saw lumber. I had help from the crew of a schooner docked nearby and from Seneca helpers. History will tell you that almost single-handedly, I cleared the land, cut and hauled logs, balanced two 150-pound millstones from Massachusetts, installed mill irons and constructed 2 water wheels. We didn't have fancy tools like you have today! We used native skill, our muscles, and a lot of determination. History will also tell you that we celebrated for 2 days. Yes, we did, with firewater and much rum.

Index

Index

Index

Auld, Hugh 172
Auld, Sophia 172, 176
Auld, Thomas 108
Avon 23, 182

B

Bailey, Harriet 104
Baltimore. *See* cities
Baptist 90, 96, 97
Barge Canal 83
Bartlett, W.H. 81
Barton, Benjamin 56
Barton, Isaac 169
Battle of Great Meadow 178
Battle of Jumonville Glen 40
Battle of Monongahela 179
Battle of Signal Hill 41
Baumfree, Isabella 136, 137. *See also* Truth, Sojourner
Baum, L. Frank 169
Bayard, Stephen 63
bears. *See* animals
beaver. *See* animals
Beaver Wars 44, 46. *See also* Iroquois Wars; Iroquois-Huron Wars; French and Iroquois Wars
Bellevue Hospital 55
Beringia. *See* Bering Land Bridge
Bering Land Bridge 13
Bible 77, 93, 97, 98, 129
Big Belly 35. *See also* Printz, Johan Björnsson
big cats. *See* animals
Billy Sunday. *See* Sunday, William Ashley
Binghamton. *See* cities
Black Rock 165, 166
Bodily, Joseph 168
Bonus Bill 78
Book of Mormon 93, 94, 95, 96, 141
Boston harbor 68
Bountiful Lumber Yard 169
Bowdoin College 123
Braddock, Edward 179
Brainerd, David 90
Bristol Massachusetts Anti-Slavery Society 177

Index

Index

Index

Index

Index

Index

Index

Index

Index

German Flatts 66
Germany 89
giant ground sloth. *See* animals; megafauna
Gist, Christopher 38
glaciations 11
glaciers 11, 12
Godwin, Joscelyn 142
Gold Bible Hill. *See* Hill Cumorah
Good Word. *See* Code of Handsome Lake
Gordon, Ann D. 131
Gore, Austin 171
Gorham, Nathaniel 50, 51, 52, 55, 163, 182
Graham, Billy 92
Grande Hermine 28
Grandin, E.B. 95, 96
Granger, Erastus 68, 69
Granger, Gideon 69
Granville. *See* counties
Great Britain 38, 40, 41, 109
Great Council 19, 20
Great Disappointment 98
Great Disease 60. *See also* Yellow Fever
Great Lakes 11, 18, 45, 61, 63, 64, 78, 104. *See also* lakes
Great Law of Peace. *See* Iroquois Confederacy
Great Meadows 40, 178. *See also* counties; Fayette
Great Peacemaker. *See* Deganaweda
Greece 118
Green-Wood Cemetery 77
Griffiths, Julia 116, 117
Groveland 101
Guadalupe 28

H

Hadley, Jonathan 95
Hagerstown. *See* cities
Hagerstown Bank 57
Haiti 118
Half Moon 29, 30
Hamilton, Alexander 63, 64
Handsome Lake 23, 24
Harlem 37
Harmony Company 8

Index

I

Index

Ice Age 1, 5, 8, 9, 10, 11, 13
igneous rock 12
Indian 16, 17, 18, 22, 23, 24, 28, 30, 31, 32, 33, 35, 36, 37, 38, 39, 40, 41, 42, 45, 46, 49, 50, 51, 52, 56, 61, 69, 93, 163, 165, 178, 180, 181, 182. *See also* Native Americans; Native American tribes
Indiana. *See* states
Inspiration Point. *See* Hill Cumorah
Inspiration Stump 141
Ireland 109
Irondequoit Creek 81
Iroquois. *See* Native American tribes
Iroquois Confederacy 18, 19, 20, 22, 43, 142, 143, 159
Iroquois-Huron War 44, 45, 46. *See also* French and Iroquois Wars
Iroquois Nation 17, 18, 19, 23, 29, 41, 44, 163
Isle LaMotte 45
Italy 116, 118

J

James Bay 30
Jaredites 94
Jefferson, Thomas 6, 42, 69, 70, 71, 72, 73, 91
Jemimakins 141
Jemison, Mary 181
Jesuits 44, 45, 167
Jikohnsaseh 18
Johnson, Elisha 57
Johnson, Nathan 176
Johnson, Polly 176
Jones, Catherine 77
Joseph Ellicott 54, 55
Journal of Major George Washington 39
Juliano, Mike 144

K

Kaysville Canning Factory 169
Kettavong, Pepsy 109
Kings
  Francis I 27, 28
  George III 41
  Louis XIV 44
  Louis XV 41

Index

Index

Index

Index

Index

Index

Index

Index

Index

Index

Index

Index

Index

Index

Watson, Elkanah 63
Webster, Ephraim 167
Weed, Thurlow 95
Weighlock Building 169
Wendat 45, 46. *See also* People of the Penninsula
Wesleyan Chapel 127
Westchester. *See* counties
Western Inland Lock and Navigation Company 63, 64
Western Inland Lock and Navigation Company, 63, 64
Western Inland Lock Navigation Company 66, 67, 72, 74, 75
West India Company 31, 35
  Dutch 35
  Swedish 35
Westmoreland. *See* counties
Weston, William 74
Wheelock, Eleazar 90
Whig party 51
White, G. Edward 32
Wilkeson, Samuel 166
Wilkinson, Jemima 141
Williamson, Charles 56
Williams, Ted 143
Wiltwyck 31. *See also* cities; Kingston
Winfield, Mason 142, 143
wolves. *See* animals
Woman's Bible 129
Women's Educational and Industrial Union 131
Women's Rights 90, 99, 108, 109, 119, 123, 125, 127, 128, 129, 131, 132, 133, 134, 136, 137
Women's Rights National Historical Park 130
women's suffrage movement 111, 128, 133, 177
Wonderful Wizard of Oz 169
Wood Creek 64, 66
Woodlawn Cemetery 130
woolly mammoth. *See* mammoths
World Anti-Slavery Convention 127, 133
Wright 74, 75
Wright, Benjamin 74, 75
Wyandot. *See also* Native American tribes; Huron

Y

Yellow Fever 60. *See also* Great Disease

Index

CPSIA information can be obtained at www.ICGtesting.com
Printed in the USA
BVOW08s0601030216

435167BV00006B/2/P